# THE IDEAL SEMINARY

Other Books by Carnegie Samuel Calian

*Today's Pastor in Tomorrow's World (revised edition)*

*The Significance of Eschatology
in the Thoughts of Nicolas Berdyaev*

*Berdyaev's Philosophy of Hope* (revised edition)

*Icon and Pulpit: The Protestant-Orthodox Encounter*

*Grace, Guts and Goods: How to Stay
Christian in an Affluent Society*

*The Gospel According to the Wall Street Journal*

*For All Your Seasons: Biblical
Directions through Life's Passages*

*Where's the Passion for Excellence in the Church?*

*Theology Without Boundaries: Encounters
of Eastern Orthodoxy and Western Tradition*

*Survival or Revival: Ten Keys to Church Vitality*

# THE IDEAL SEMINARY

## Pursuing Excellence in Theological Education

Carnegie Samuel Calian

Westminster John Knox Press
LOUISVILLE
LONDON ·LEIDEN

*Book design by Teri Vinson*
*Cover design by Pam Poll Graphic Design*

Published by Westminster John Knox Press
Louisville, Kentucky

This book is printed on acid-free paper that meets the American National Standards Institute Z39.48 standard. ∞

PRINTED IN THE UNITED STATES OF AMERICA

02 03 04 05 06 07 08 09 10 11 — 10 9 8 7 6 5 4 3 2 1

**Library of Congress Cataloging-in-Publication Data**

Calian, Carnegie Samuel.
    The ideal seminary : pursuing excellence in theological education / by Carnegie Samuel Calian.
      p. cm.
    Includes bibliographical references and index.
    ISBN 0-664-22266-8 (alk. paper)
      1. Theological seminaries. 2. Theology—Study and teaching. I. Title.

BV4020 .C35 2001
230'.071'1—dc21

            2001026844

Dedicated to the members of Pittsburgh Seminary's Board of Directors for their commitment to graduate theological education on behalf of the church and society with particular appreciation to the chairs of our board during the past twenty years of my presidency of the seminary:

Henry C. Herchenroether Jr.   James E. Lee
Robert C. Holland             Laird Stuart
Nathan Pearson                Edwin V. Clarke Jr.
Marianne Wolfe                Robert T. Harper

"Teacher, which commandment in the law is the greatest?" He said to him, " 'You shall love the Lord your God with all your heart, and with all your soul, and with all your mind.' This is the greatest and first commandment."
> —Theological Education according to Jesus (Matthew 22:36–38)

If institutional reality could be remade to heart's desire, what would the *ideal theological school* be like? (italics added)
> —*To Understand God Truly: What's Theological about a Theological School?* by David H. Kelsey (Westminster John Knox Press)

Albert Einstein said, "We cannot solve the problems we have created with the same thinking that created them." We might modify his quote slightly and say for our purposes, "We are unable to solve the problems we have created with the same theologizing and church [*and seminary*] practices that have created them." (italics added)
> —*Survival or Revival: Ten Keys to Church Vitality* by C. S. Calian (Westminster John Knox Press)

# CONTENTS

# PREFACE

*I* wrote this book to celebrate my past twenty years as President and Professor of Theology at Pittsburgh Theological Seminary. I accepted the invitation from Pittsburgh as a direction from God and ventured forth on February 1, 1981. Through the years I have come to owe a tremendous debt of gratitude to my colleagues—trustees, faculty, administrators, staff, students, alums, donors, clergy, and the countless church members who have also served as colleagues to me knowingly and unknowingly. Leadership in theological education is a team endeavor from beginning to end; seminary education will always be a work in progress and will never measure up to everyone's satisfaction, including mine.

Above all, theological education is for the sake of equipping and nurturing the people of God to witness faithfully and cogently in the world to the One who loves us beyond our comprehension. The most faithful theology we can teach is summed up in our doxology before God whose majesty and mystery exceeds our imagination and formulation. To learn to love God truly and passionately is the goal of theological education.

This book is designed to address all parties who have a stake in theological schools and who wish to enhance the role and influence of these schools among our churches and communities. Present as well as potential students will find this volume useful; hopefully it will provide reflective material for all members of the seminary community. *Discussion Starters* at the end of each chapter are there to stir the reader's imagination and offer added suggestions on our way to the ideal seminary. This book might also serve as a useful catalyst for on-campus and cyber-campus retreats at the opening of a school year, engaging all the stakeholders concerned with seminary education to think theologically as well as organizationally on the aim of theological schools as we seek to create a common unity of purpose and understanding of our mission.

One key idea I emphasize is to create a shared vision of ownership of theological education for the people of God. We need also to enlarge the base of qualified participants who think about graduate theological education; that is, to shift from our present predominately "clerical paradigm" to a "people of God paradigm." In all aspects of theological education, we need to pursue excellence as we seek to educate our congregations and community to regain their passion for service and mutual trust. God entered our humanity demonstrating and teaching forgiving love; the task of theological education is to articulate the forgiveness embodied in Jesus the Christ before the forces of darkness seeking to deny us our authentic humanity and birthright.

As we journey together through the complex culture of theological education, I welcome your comments. Hopefully together we will have a better focus on *the ideal seminary.* Whether or not we arrive at that ideal goal, the journey itself has its own intrinsic rewards for every learning community of believers who is seeking God's will and wisdom to save us from dehumanizing ourselves; that is, diminishing the image of God in one another. This is what happens when we reject the centrality of God in our lives, either denying or ignoring the fact that in life and in death we belong to God—to settle for any lesser outlook than this is to cheat ourselves. Theological education is dedicated to recovering our divine birthright and to experiencing lasting fulfillment in God who expects our total devotion without reservation.

To connect with me, my seminary and e-mail addresses are: 616 North Highland Avenue, Pittsburgh, PA 15206-2596; calian@pts.edu.

Introduction

# WHY SEMINARY EDUCATION?

*H*ave you caught yourself confusing the word "seminary" with "cemetery" and then joking about it? I have heard that quip on occasion as individuals seek to get a rise out of me. Perhaps there is a greater link between seminaries and cemeteries than we are willing to admit to ourselves. There may also be lessons that seminary communities can learn from cemeteries.

The word "seminary" is from the Latin *seminarium*, meaning "seed plot," and suggests a place where something is bred, grown, or developed—namely a "hot house" for plants. In the medieval period it was used by the church as the designation for settings where candidates for the priesthood could be nourished and formed in their sacred calling apart from distracting "worldly" influences. The seminary was to be a perpetual seed plot for preparing seminarians to be formed into ministers of God within a sheltered environment, like young plants in a hot house—appropriate, since the church often recruited young candidates for the priesthood from the age of twelve.

Today, in North America, "seminary" (or theological seminary) is one of several terms for those institutions that provide post-baccalaureate education for men and women for a variety of ministries in churches and related agencies. It should be noted that in the past among Protestants the term "seminary" was not limited to theological education but was also applied to various preparatory schools and colleges, especially those designed for women. One of the earlier and perhaps better known of these schools is now coeducational; it is the Friends Seminary in New York City, founded in 1786, for young people from kindergarten through grade twelve.

In the 1780s most Protestant clergy received a liberal arts education in log house colleges that later developed into universities, followed by an apprenticeship of six months to a year during which one "read divinity" with an ordained clergyman. Concern for the adequacy and accountability of such preparation led to the formation of seminaries by churches beginning with the Reformed Theological Seminary in New Brunswick, New Jersey, in 1784; Saint Mary's Seminary in Baltimore, Maryland, in 1791; the antecedent of

Pittsburgh Theological Seminary (known then as Service Seminary) in 1794; Andover Newton Theological Seminary in 1807; followed by Princeton and Union Theological (Virginia) Seminaries in 1812. All of the above mentioned seminaries are included today among the 243 accredited schools of the Association of Theological Schools (ATS) in the United States and Canada embracing Protestant, Orthodox, and Catholic traditions.

Seminaries were founded and continue to thrive in order to provide passionate and competent leadership for the ongoing renewal and outreach of the churches. Issues of decline in the church's influence and membership have been a constant concern for every generation of believers. Some have observed in every era that the church is only a generation from extinction. This of course could be more abundantly illustrated if there were no endowed churches. The confusion between seminaries and cemeteries may be no laughing matter. Actually, there are lessons to be learned from cemeteries for seminaries and churches.

First, in this death-denying culture of ours,[1] *death's reality highlights our finitude*. To put it boldly before us, *we are born to die*; it is within the years intervening between birth and death that the significant questions of life are raised: What can we know? What do we do with moral dilemmas? What can we hope for?

When God is factored into our responses to these questions, we become budding theologians whether or not we acknowledge that fact to ourselves. Our quest for answers has brought many of us to the seminary; seminaries ought to be safe places where we have the opportunity to wrestle with these issues. Part of our theological search at the seminary also involves us in listening to one another's story, each person's faith journey. Theologizing is reflecting on each of our stories. Whose theology is more pure and right will depend upon a careful weighing of our biases vis-à-vis our understanding of scripture as we call upon the Holy Spirit to lead us into truth. And guess what? The Holy Spirit does indeed inform and guide us through the study of scripture. John Calvin rightly taught his students that scripture is the school of the Holy Spirit.

Further direction and support are given as we gain a historical perspective—cemeteries can provide us with this valuable in-depth perspective. With the assistance of competent interpretation from scholars of history, we learn of the possible pitfalls and joys ahead of us. There are many lessons buried in the past waiting to be discovered. Parker J. Palmer expresses it so well in these words: "Learning to speak and listen in that invisible community of history and thought makes one's world immeasurably larger and forever changes one's life."[2]

From the vantage point of the cemetery, I believe there is much to be learned from the "communion of saints," although no curriculum could capture it in three or even six years. We are born not only to die, but also to study until we enter death's door. From my standpoint, studying is an essential part of our stewardship to God. There is so much knowledge that takes us beyond our limited horizons and saves us from the fads and tendencies that constrict us to dogmatic answers, denying us our God-given exercise of creativity.

Second, cemeteries not only make us aware of our finitude in time and place, but *cemeteries also convey to us the need for urgency and sacrifice throughout our faith journey.* Those of us who have encountered death can speak from experience as to how it interrupts lives, causes despair and even violence. An encounter with death is like a recurring nightmare (or dream) that doesn't disappear after you wake up and brush your teeth in the morning. It is like a gray cloud hanging over us and affecting everyone within our intimate circle of family and friends. I have had two such brushes with death and for reasons known only to God I have survived, but I have not been left untouched. Each encounter energized and transformed me to live more fully. These encounters with death have reminded me that we live on borrowed time. You and I have a common calling not to waste our precious and limited time on earth. Our Lord expects us to serve, not to bury those unique talents God has bestowed upon each of us. Unfortunately, this truth is lost upon many who find themselves among the walking dead in our society, no longer energized by a meaningful purpose that gives life zest and excitement.

Each time I visit the cemetery or participate in a memorial service, I am tempted to ask the question "why?" or "why not me?" There are never satisfactory answers to the question of why; the lack of answers confronts us with mystery and the unexplainable. Cemeteries inform seminary communities that they may not have all the answers to life's mysteries. In actuality, we may have very few answers at all. Cemeteries force us to be silent, as painful as that might be. It seems we are left with our unanswered prayers. We are reminded again and again that ours is a walk of faith, not certainties. We live from grace to grace, from mercy to mercy, every moment of our lives; we have no other guarantees in life. This is God's way of keeping in touch with us. It also keeps us from proclaiming our theologies too dogmatically, claiming more than we can substantiate. All of us are capable of theological malpractice.

This is not to say that we shouldn't maintain convictions, such as my faith in the resurrection of Christ. Such a conviction extends beyond rational explanation. To acknowledge this is to say that even within the community of faith there exists more questions than answers during this earthly pilgrimage of ours. Such an admission calls for a large measure of humility among students and faculty studying the sacred text. We find ourselves reading and re-reading with awe and admiration the sacrifices of those who have gone before and whose foundations have made it possible for us to embark on our journey of faith.

Third, the cemetery teaches the seminary community that *our culture of death need not be the last word on our existence*. The human spirit is greater than its bodily presence. While we cannot, any of us, outrun the temporal realities of physical death and separation, the seminary community centered in Christ witnesses to the reality of transforming life—the Christian faith rests its case on resurrection hope (1 Corinthians 15:1–28).

The seminary is a school of hope, not a school of death. In fact, the seminary curriculum through its varied disciplines probes all kinds of issues associated with today's cemetery, namely the experience of dying and death, violence, tragedy, injustice, and countless other unanswered questions regarding this world. While it is true that everything depends on the lens through which we view the world, in seminary we learn to wear a theological lens that enables us to see beyond the limits of empirical constrictions. So often our theories and theologies dictate what we see and don't see. We must be on guard, therefore, against those viewpoints and beliefs that cater only to our biases and limited comprehension.

As biblically educated Christians, we believe that the death of Jesus is a way of encountering what is wrong with our world. The cross of Christ reminds us that death is like a terrorist intrusion; it is a violent experience even when we expect it. Christian faith confronts death. For instance, all four of our Gospel narratives—Matthew, Mark, Luke, and John—are primarily death stories, passion stories. It has been estimated that one-fourth of Matthew's Gospel emphasizes death's reality, one-third of Mark's Gospel, at least one-fifth of Luke's account, and nearly one-half of John's Gospel. We have more details on the death of Jesus than any other aspect of his brief earthly life. In short, the good news of the New Testament is placed within the context of death. The resurrection of Christ is a response to this culture of death; the grace of God does prevail over the graves at the cemetery.

This fact was vividly illustrated for me when I participated some years ago in a Russian Orthodox Easter celebration in Paris.[3] Following the sacred midnight celebration of a Russian Orthodox Easter, the faithful gathered the next afternoon at the cemetery for a vesper service. The priest led the believers from the chapel to the rows of graves with loved ones standing nearby and announced dramatically, "*Christos voskres*" ("Christ is risen!"). The family members standing by the cemetery plots responded with enthused voices "*Voistinno voskres*" ("He is risen indeed!"). In the face of the realities of the cemetery, the Christian seminary teaches the resurrection of Christ. Perhaps we could appreciate this message more fully if we would hold some seminary classes at the cemetery to remind us of the empowering significance of our resurrection faith. Christian faith does not run from the realities of life—it gives hope in the midst of dying and death. And yet, nothing can lock out death; even the bank's steel vault cannot lock out death. Death is inevitable; and it is there at the end of everyone's earthly pilgrimage. But the ultimate reality, we believe, is that divine grace extends beyond the grave; it is this good news that we are privileged to study and proclaim at the seminary. This is our hope, no matter how imperfectly we express it to those around us.

Isn't this the final intent of seminary education, namely, to share our faith? We are being theologically educated in order to share our faith more fully. Everything we learn at seminary is for someone else. Do we need to be reminded that we can't share it well if we haven't studied it adequately? The aim of seminary education is not simply to produce an educated clergy, but even more so to build up the people of God, to become an educated congregation in Christ.[4] The practice of learning is for the purpose of giving hope to others.

Our discussions in the following pages are divided into three parts—*first, institutional challenges* facing theological schools in the area of leadership, community life, governance, tenure, and academic freedom are highlighted. *Second, programmatic challenges* are centered in the schools' self-understanding of their purpose expressed in the curriculum and how this is linked to the mission of local churches. These issues are further complicated by the realities of globalization and multiculturalism. Suggestions are also offered for expanding the services and programs of theological education to a wider audience. In the *third and final part of the book, attention is given to student concerns* as potential candidates for ministry re-evaluate their calling and qualifications for ministry. What happens to one's faith in the educational process, the importance of prayer and spiritual formation, and an outline of characteristics for the ideal seminary are given. Not until the Afterword is there a brief discussion of seminary finances. This is not because of its insignificance, but because we become too preoccupied with the realities of funding theological education that oftentimes our purpose for existing is neglected.

Every chapter ends with "discussion starters" to encourage the reader to interact with other interested parties as we seek together to build the ideal seminary for the new millennium. Our discussion commences with a focus on the relationship of seminary education and the need for church leadership at the grassroots.

# PART I   Institutional Challenges

# Chapter 1

# Seminary Education and Leadership

*T*he following abbreviated mission and purpose statements, from three traditional denominational seminaries, refer to leadership, both implicitly and explicitly:

> *Luther Seminary*—St. Paul, Minnesota (Evangelical Lutheran Church in America) ". . . educates leaders for Christian communities called and sent by the Holy Spirit to witness to salvation through Jesus Christ and to serve in God's world."
>
> *Garrett-Evangelical Theological Seminary*—Evanston, Illinois (United Methodist) "To know God in Christ and, through preparing spiritual leaders, to help others to know God in Christ."
>
> *Pittsburgh Theological Seminary*—Pittsburgh, Pennsylvania (Presbyterian Church, U.S.A.) ". . . we seek to prepare men and women for pastoral ministry and Christian lay leadership in all phases of the Church's outreach."

Nowhere do these schools, or for that matter the accrediting standards of the Association of Theological Schools, define what leadership is.[1] *If the task of theological education is leadership education, then what exactly is the profile of a church leader upon which we can agree?* Do seminaries really see themselves in the business of leadership education? Or is it our task simply to polish the inherent leadership abilities that individuals already possess? To what extent do theological schools actually shape leadership, or is leadership primarily a gift certain persons possess? Is it the seminary's task to create Christian leaders, molding and designing according to the biases of faculty, staff, and the school's ecclesiastical heritage? Do we see ourselves developing leaders through our teaching efforts? For that matter, have we ever invited our students to think of themselves as leaders regardless of how ordinary they might feel? Or is the biblical understanding of discipleship focused perhaps more on followership than leadership?

To what extent is it our duty to raise student awareness regarding the nature and responsibility of leadership? Are we as theological educators ready for the awesome challenge to graduate seminarians who will make a significant leadership difference in our churches and communities? And if we were to give ourselves a grade on how well we are presently executing this task, would we pass or fail?

Frankly, I am not sure whether during the accreditation process that theological schools undergo, anyone considers it the schools' responsibility to plan how to graduate leaders who will make a difference among our churches and communities. Our resolve should be to foster wise leaders to renew congregations and communities. Daniel O. Aleshire, executive director of the Association of Theological Schools, shared his concern at the 2000 biennial meeting of the ATS when he repeated a question raised by a neurosurgeon friend: "Do theological schools know how to educate people for the jobs they are going to do when they graduate?"[2] Aleshire believes that this is a fair question. "If beginning surgeons had the equivalent amount of skill for their profession that theological graduates have for theirs, would you go to one for surgery? This neurosurgeon believes that the church is as important a place as the operating room."[3] For us, the minister, as the spiritual physician, is the grassroots theologian in charge. Do our graduates have a sufficiently clear vision of leadership for ministry? Leadership malpractice is unfortunately widespread today in our churches, far more than many of us may be willing to admit. For seminaries and divinity schools to graduate grassroots theologians who have not grasped how to lead is a serious matter that can no longer be ignored by faculties, administrators, and trustees.

## Churches in Need of Leadership

Is church leadership really a neglected discussion topic on our campuses? We seem to be preoccupied with other agenda: our conversations tend to focus on controversial issues, theological differences, personalities, and sports. We might complain at times about church leadership and its shortcomings, but have we developed a theology of leadership for ourselves? Can we as the people of God establish a common understanding of leadership in spite of our theological and philosophical differences? The need to nurture leaders in our churches can wait no longer. For the past several decades, most denominations have been downsizing themselves to death. Who is going to stem this downward trend? The leadership crunch among churches affects us all—conservatives, liberals, and moderates. Even the so-called megachurches are in search of a sustaining formula for effective leadership that promises future growth for their churches.

According to Donald E. Miller, sociologist at the University of Southern California and author of *Reinventing American Protestantism: Christianity in the New Millennium*,[4] our future is bleak. In a recent "reality retreat" with Presbyterian seminary presidents and chairs of their Boards of Directors, Miller informed us that "in twenty-five years (2025), most mainline churches will be bankrupt (spiritually, numerically, and financially), unable to reinvigorate themselves with today's median church membership at fifty-five years of age and rising." At the same time, he reported that "Christianity itself will be very vital in 2025, but without the driving force of mainline churches."[5] As a realistic optimist, I refuse to accept such a gloomy projection as inevitable.

Theological schools that are connected to churches and denominations need to rethink and refocus our educational program and make a more concerted effort to educate future leaders who will make a difference. Our efforts should also be directed toward identifying potential leaders among the laity as well as candidates for the clergy. Once these students are enrolled in classes, we need to assist them by developing theologies of leadership within the courses of our curriculum. The making of a Christian leader is complex, and there is no single theological formula or infallible guru we can study and emulate as we navigate through the leadership conflicts before us. Nevertheless, we need articulate leaders of faith who can offer hope to a society seeking to restore its trust in God. In other words, we want leaders who can think and lead *inside* the church as well as leaders who can think and lead *outside* of the church and within our communities. Seminary education should call us to wrestle honestly with the question of effective and ineffective leadership, to dig more deeply into our traditions for examples, and through a process of dialogue to shape new paradigms of leadership to empower the people of God into a renewed partnership with God. Clergy and laity need a shared vision of a common apostolate—that is to say, a common calling and commissioning to go forth together as God's people who are interdependent. We need to progress with sensitivity and compassion as exemplified by Jesus and no longer be limited to a professional "clerical paradigm" that has divided us into a church of clergy and a church of laity. We must recover the Reformation spirit to be *one people under God*. The apostle Paul, encouraged by his own tent-making vocation, abandoned the false dichotomy separating us into a two-tier Christianity—clergy and laity—and by his leadership example testified to our oneness as the people of God (Galatians 3:28).

To what extent are seminaries prepared to promote single-class Christianity—to enable clergy and laity to be equal beneficiaries of theological education? Unfortunately, the prevailing mode in most theological schools is the "clerical paradigm," which promotes theological wisdom as simply clergy education, not normally directed to the laity. But is it right for theological wisdom to be so limited? Theological pedagogy that is open to all God's people will enable seminaries and divinity schools to educate more inclusively and to reduce the spiritual illiteracy that exists at the grassroots today. A graduate theological program of learning for all God's people who qualify will create new alliances and widen the circle of potential leaders who can trust and respect one another's perspective as they work together to advance the kingdom of God. The church is too important to be entrusted solely to either clergy or laity in isolation. Refocusing theological schools and their limited resources to support not only the clergy, but all of God's people who qualify, will be an important way to address the leadership shortage in the church. That leadership crisis is, I believe, primarily an educational crisis. Therefore, theological schools ought to welcome qualified laity to study with their clergy-to-be brothers and sisters in our goal to be partners in ministry. The new partnership with God's people must be built on a common language and a mature respect for one another's calling in life.

## Theological Education
## as Leadership Education

Theological schools of every tradition are not simply graduate schools where we learn to think theologically, but also graduate schools of leadership. According to Aleshire, "leadership involves the art of helping an organization to continue its best practices and commitments while cultivating the imagination necessary to envision the changes that will advance the cause of the organization's vocation."[6] Seminary communities as well as churches "need leadership that simultaneously keeps faith with the past and puts faith in the future, leadership that is as sensitive to deep traditions as to profound change."[7] Seminaries and churches require leaders who are willing to be educated in the context of continuity and change, a never-ending tension that faces every generation of believers.

How should future church leaders respond to the voices of continuity and the voices of change confronting them at every turn? There is no curriculum or single course that we can offer to guarantee that our students will become successful leaders. Educating for Christian leadership begins first and foremost with one's own spiritual journey for self-understanding before God. Through courses on spiritual formation, students gain insight as they face their journey of faith. Spiritual self-understanding is nurtured by critical reflection in the historical, biblical, theological, and ethical courses of the curriculum. Concurrently and most important, prayer synthesizes the spiritual and critical dimensions of one's reflections through engagements in ministry, strengthened by constructive feedback in community.

Our educational process offers content and skills to aid one's calling for leadership and service in the world, fueling the Spirit's flame within us to be God's disciples wherever the holy winds of Pentecost direct us. God's passionate call of redemption centered in Christ is our unfailing beacon of hope in this changing world of ours.

## Leadership Styles

Only leaders who truly believe in the living Source of hope can make a difference in churches and communities; how this hope is expressed points us to various styles of leadership. In our theological schools, these styles of leadership are practiced by faculty, staff, adjuncts, and pastors who serve as field supervisors and mentors off-campus. We are oftentimes emulating one style of leadership or another and are not always aware we are doing so. It can also be said that among theological schools, some styles of leadership are encouraged over others.[8] Our aim above all as leaders is to be motivated to nurture relationships that lead to respect and love for one another. It takes leadership to build communities of hope in the name of Christ; this building process requires keen awareness, then, of our leadership styles.

Professor Daniel Goleman of Rutgers University has identified six styles of leadership; each has strengths and shortcomings.[9] There are *coercive* leaders who demand immediate compliance. Although certain life or death crises in an organization may require such action, the downside to coercive leadership practices is that they undermine motivation and morale and severely limit flexibility within the organization. The medicine of coercion applied to a sick organization often runs the danger of killing rather than saving it. Goleman does not recommend this form. However, there are unfortunately religious groups (like cults) that are organized around coercive practices and fear.

Second, there is *authoritative* leadership, which tends to mobilize people toward a vision, especially when confusion and insecurity prevail. Faculty as well as administrators practice this form of leadership when teaching or articulating the mission of the institution. Authoritative leadership assumes that there is a certain earned expertise that inspires respect. There are times when leadership calls for contributing authoritative clarity and informed explanations where there was ignorance and a desire for understanding.

Authoritative leaders must be willing to receive feedback and criticism from students and colleagues. Authoritative leadership that is too defensive has an unhealthy tendency to become coercive in practice. Constructive criticism will give the organization, the classroom, or the community the free-dom to innovate, experiment, and take calculated risks to further its mission. Hopefully, the checks and balances in most organizations will enable author-itative leadership to operate in a healthy environment.

Third, there is *affiliative* leadership, which does not say, "Do what I say!" but rather, "People come first." The affiliative leader places priority on the values and feelings of others rather than on tasks or goals. This kind of lead-ership listens to the emotions of others and is skilled in working for harmony among members of the community. Reality for the affiliative leader resides in relationships, building strong emotional bonds. An affiliative attitude in lead-ership seeks to turn an organization into a supportive community of friends. In such an atmosphere, flexibility is heightened, and positive feedback is encouraged. Everyone assumes leadership responsibility as we each work for a sense of belonging.

The downside of this upbeat and affirming approach is that it can diminish people's willingness to criticize in the face of poor performance, leading to uncorrected and mediocre performance. Are Christian leaders too tolerant today of mediocrity in our seminaries and churches? Have we lost our Pauline passion for excellence before God? Have we in our desire to affirm one another failed to provide clear directives and discipline to navigate through the numerous temptations facing us? As Goleman reminds us, the affiliative style leaves many organizations rudderless. Has this been the practice among numerous non-profit organizations of good will, including our churches and theological schools? Have we become so process-oriented that our perfor-mance has suffered, doing more harm than good to others? An affiliative style of leadership by itself can lead an organization to failure. As Goleman suggests, "Authoritative leaders state a mission, set standards, and let people know how their work is furthering the group's goals. Alternate that with the caring, nurturing approach of the affiliative leader and you have a potent combination."[10]

Fourth, there is the *democratic* style of leadership, which is an excellent approach when there is time for consensus building to discuss the options before a decision needs to be made. Take the case of Sister Mary, who ran a Catholic school in a large metropolitan area that was threatened with closure. After years of losing money, the school was slated for closing by the arch-diocese. Sister Mary wisely called a meeting of all parties involved—teach-ers, staff, parents, and community leaders. She asked for advice and suggestions in the face of the pending decision. After two months of meet-ings, a consensus was clear: the school would have to be closed. "People mourned the loss of the school, but they understood its inevitability. Virtually no one objected."[11] In contrast, at another Catholic school the priest in charge acted by fiat, without any democratic processing of the situation. The reaction was violent, with lawsuits and harsh, broken relationships.

Democratic leadership is necessary, but we must be prepared to take time for the required processing. On the other hand, leadership by democracy is sometimes abused by endless meetings and leaders who defer crucial decision-making. Frustration builds up and people feel confused and leaderless. How often has this been the case with church-related organizations? Poor application of the democratic process can escalate conflicts. Democratic leadership works best when the leader is willing to take a direction. "And it almost goes without saying that building consensus is wrong-headed in times of crisis."[12] There are serious situations when there is not the time to process the matter properly. On such occasions, a swift judgment is required; the leader must pray and seek Solomon's wisdom through listening with an understanding heart and exercising wise discernment. Ultimately, the practice of leadership is an art rather than a science, and Christian leaders ought to have a keen appreciation for what it means to be led by the Spirit of God in all circumstances (Psalm 32:8).

Fifth, there is also the *pacesetting* style of leadership, whereby the head of the organization expects excellence and self-direction that points to high standards. Its application, warns Goleman, should be used sparingly, however. Why? Because the leader makes demands that overwhelm members of the community, causing everyone's morale to fall, and the leader's real expectations are at times not clear. In fact, one can feel too stupid to ask. We seem to forget that there are often more dumb answers than dumb questions. As a result, trust breaks down. Work no longer becomes a matter of doing one's best, but of trying to second-guess what the leader wants.[13] This type of leadership lacks adequate feedback and members feel disempowered in the process. The pacesetting type of leadership fails to reach its goals, which could have been better realized through dialogue in a context of mutual respect. And yet, this type of leadership has its place among highly motivated, competent persons who have self-confidence and like to be left alone with a pacesetting target. This situation is no doubt true in research institutions and the computer industry where pacesetting leadership abounds.

Sixth and last, there is the *coaching* style of leadership, within which one acts like a counselor more than a professor or administrator, listening carefully and with a sense of genuine concern to help others see change as an opportunity for growth. The coaching style can assist congregations and seminary communities to identify the unique strengths and weaknesses of their members. It is through this process that one learns to link personal ambitions and institutional aspirations. Servant leadership is another form of coaching that demonstrates support for the benefit of others. Seminary faculty and staff, as well as pastors and students who practice a coaching style of leadership will excel at delegating responsibility and giving permission to others to be imaginative, creative, and even to make mistakes in their long-term development of discipleship before God. A coaching style of leadership says to the follower, "I believe in you and I expect your best efforts."[14]

I believe that theological education that exemplifies through its faculty, staff, students, and trustees authoritative, affiliative, democratic, and coaching styles of leadership will model for our churches and communities invaluable lessons on leadership. As leaders, we will also learn to switch flexibly among the leadership styles as needed. All of us who wish to belong to learning communities, and hopefully this is true of all churches and theological schools, will accept the challenge to become leaders who, by the grace of God, will make a meaningful difference in ministry because our hearts, minds, and souls are "in sync" as we offer our prayers of thanksgiving to God.

## Grassroots Theologians Becoming Leaders

Theological schools as learning communities need to cultivate an attitude for leadership informed by the curriculum and through our worship times together. In practice, we ought to follow those styles of leadership that are in keeping with our faith principles. Wise leaders will consider carefully and prayerfully the trade-offs involved in every decision-making situation. Wise pastor-theologians will be those who have gained not only spiritual self-awareness, but also social awareness of the neighborhoods where they practice ministry. The grassroots theologian who has not been given the opportunity to discuss and reflect upon leadership with faculty and administrators will be ill-equipped to connect effectively with congregations seeking renewal. For this purpose, theological schools might consider introducing a three- to four-day "Senior Class Retreat" on Christian leadership that involves faculty, experienced clergy, and lay leaders through a process that integrates the contents of the curriculum from the standpoint of leadership. This could be done effectively through the means of case studies on leadership. By consciously linking together the contents of the curriculum to case studies, grassroots theologians of tomorrow might be in a better position to formulate the beginnings of a theology for leadership for themselves that addresses creatively the tension between continuity and change, which is the underlying cause behind many of today's conflicts within our churches, cities, and neighborhoods. Through such a reflective retreat, we can help graduating seniors begin to link their seminary education with the leadership wisdom so necessary for their practice of ministry. A senior class retreat on leadership is a starting point for highlighting the importance of leadership and will enhance the contribution and relevance of theological education to our churches and communities.

## DISCUSSION STARTER

*M*any faculty and administrators believe the curriculum in their schools is already so crowded with required and elective courses that including courses on leadership is not feasible. There is also the perennial discussion about extending the formal three-year study period of full-time students and adding a fourth year of study. This, of course, would create its own set of problems for students in debt and complicate their family considerations. Perhaps another approach that could unite parishioners and theological schools in their common concern to enhance leadership in ministry would be a specially designed program on leadership after graduation and ordination.

Perhaps a *two-year mentorship program in Christian leadership* could be introduced following ordination into one's tradition, leading to a certificate on leadership from an accredited theological school. The newly ordained person would enroll in this mentorship program at a seminary near to his or her place of ministry (and preferably not the alma mater) where a special ecumenical team would mentor a group of newly ordained clergy through a standardized program designed and approved by the Association of Theological Schools[15] to assure appropriate and uniform standards. I envision adding a staff member to the Association assigned to organize and guide this important transition period from formal studies into the first two years of one's practice of ministry.

Each team could consist of an experienced pastor respected for his or her leadership in ministry, a faculty member who could contribute effectively regardless of field of expertise, an institutional chaplain knowledgeable in non-parish ministries, and a layperson who can ably represent the pew and the needs of laity. Regular team meetings with the newly ordained clergy would be scheduled, perhaps quarterly. Annually, for one week of every year, the newly ordained and mentorship team will take up residence on a seminary campus and review the past year's ministry. Someone from the ecumenical team will track each newly ordained person in the practice of ministry prior to the retreat. In the first year, a specialist in organizational behavior and leadership might instruct the group and assist the newly ordained clergy as needed. In the second year, a sociologist who understands churches and communities could be invited for input and interaction with the group. Through such a process, the newly ordained could further enhance their leadership skills while gaining personal awareness and insight into the complex context in which they are called to minister. This two-year mentorship period will also provide ecumenical bonding that will prove to be supportive in future years.

Funding for such a project could come from denominations and interested foundations. On a trial basis, this proposal might be administered by the ATS. The program could be tested in one or two regions and improved upon as a pilot project before expanding nationally. By itself, this proposal is not a panacea for the leadership crisis before us, but it can serve as a constructive step forward in addressing a serious ecumenical concern. What are your thoughts on this proposal? Should the leadership program be voluntary or required by each denomination? Failure to implement an intentional program on leadership will further endanger the future of our churches already suffering from inadequate leadership. Without strong support for our graduates, members of congregations may seek their own validation process for ordination, ignoring the requirement of an M.Div. degree.

Chapter 2

# The Search for Excellence
# among Theological Schools

*H*ow theological schools are viewed in the marketplace does matter! It influences our competitive bid for financial resources and the recruitment of well-qualified students and personnel. The competition to be well regarded and excellent is keen among the schools. Of course, the leadership performance of our graduates in churches and in the public arena reinforces positively or negatively the impressions others hold of our schools. Every accredited theological institution wishes to be seen in the best light possible. How, then, do we determine the criteria for the top theological schools offering a Master of Divinity degree, the academic degree most in demand among theological students?

### Which Are the Top Theological Schools?

For instance, is it possible to ascertain the top ten theological schools in North America that offer the M.Div. diploma? There are published lists of top professional schools in the fields of law, medicine, engineering, and business administration, for example. These lists are usually based on the preferences of deans of professional schools who vote anonymously. For potential candidates entering these professional schools, it becomes a factor of pride to be accepted by one of the ten top schools. It is also a source of recognition and self-esteem for the institutions, graduates, and donors.[1]

To the best of my knowledge, however, there has been no ranking of theological seminaries and divinity schools that grant basic professional degrees such as the Master of Divinity, the Master of Arts in Religious Education, and the Doctor of Ministry degrees. There was published in the late sixties a ranking of seminaries and divinity schools which offered the earned doctorates (Ph.D. or Th.D.).[2] Since then, an incomplete research ranking for the Ph.D. degree has been made by the National Research Council, but still none that includes the primary professional degree (M.Div.).[3] I consulted the Association of Theological Schools in the United States and Canada (headquartered in Pittsburgh, Pennsylvania) for verification of my observations and found that indeed no such survey on institutions granting the first professional degrees has ever been made. In answer to my "Why not?" the immediate response was, "What would be the criteria?"

Perhaps the selection of the top schools would be bogged down with theological and ideological biases and no clear-cut consensus could be reached. Of course, there are measurable criteria for academic excellence: library holdings, number of earned doctorates among faculty members, faculty/student ratio, publications by faculty, financial resources, adequacy of facilities, quality of teaching, extracurricular programs on campus, the transcripts of students, and the sufficiency of the administrative staff and trustees. These categories are certainly important to accrediting agencies and to foundations that lend support. Could this not be the beginning point for establishing a basis for the ranking of professional schools for ministry? Or are we concerned that perhaps such a ranking might be too revealing and embarrassing to the entire theological education enterprise?

Some say that the top ten schools should be determined by the success of graduates in passing professional licensing exams and subsequent performance in the ensuing years. While professional licensing examinations in some professions are fairly standardized throughout the country and influence the content of professional education, there does not seem to be any commonly accepted set of standards for graduates of theological schools. Ordination exams, when they exist, vary among the ecclesiastical traditions, as well as within any given denomination. Also, seminarians and faculties often resist these ecclesiastical restrictions, including critical notations from accrediting agencies whom they feel do not appreciate the tradition in which their theological schools stand. It may develop in the future, due to these restrictions from the schools, that the ATS itself evolves from being principally an accrediting agency and becomes instead an "Association on Theological Education" that provides a forum or platform to facilitate theological discourse not only among schools, but related organizations on a wider interfaith basis.

Among medical schools, there is general agreement on the study of human anatomy, but among theological schools, there is much ambiguity in defining "spiritual anatomy" and, hence, what should be favored in the theological curriculum. As a consequence, the curricula of seminaries lack ecumenical consensus. The accreditation standards for theological education expect certain basic organizational norms, such as faculty to student ratios, but leave the interpretation of the curriculum to each school's ethos and tradition. There is no single interpretation as to what a biblical, christocentric, and ethical curriculum ought to comprise in theological education. In practice, it seems that the seminary curriculum—the courses and programs offered—is subject to church authorities and turf politics among faculty, making it difficult to develop a coherent plan acceptable to all the members. If the current debate on "shifting boundaries"[4] in the theological curriculum does not properly address the individual self-interests of faculty members, it will go nowhere. Perhaps this is one reason why curriculum battles once fought are left alone for many years before being revisited. This is complicated further by the wide range of starting points and experiences theological students have today. What may be seen as "healthy" theological education for some faculty and students may seem "sick" and inadequate to others. How, then, can theological educators be expected to agree on the standards needed to select the top theological institutions related to the Association of Theological Schools? Indeed, what would be the criteria?

My suspicion is that many of us—trustees, faculty, administrators, students, graduates—have a secret list of top schools. The models of theological education in our past often become the yardsticks by which we gauge our present concerns and opinions regarding programs and endeavors at our present institutions. Perhaps we need to stimulate dialogue within our respective schools by submitting our individual lists of top schools without comment and then comparing the tabulated results for discussion and debate among the constituencies of each academic community. I wonder if a common list would emerge. In addition to this process, perhaps we ought also to exercise feedback through our respective school newsletters sent to graduates, donors, and friends to elicit their opinions, perceptions, and realities, suggesting ways we could do a better job of assisting the churches and society with our limited resources. The more inclusive the input, the better position we are in to assess more effective ways to serve our seminarians and fulfill our continuing responsibilities to graduates. Such feedback is important, lest we suffer from a *narrowness of vision* with limited conversations among ourselves. Academia at times has a tendency toward limited monologue while it complains about the lack of communication; we often overlook the fact that individual responsibility for listening to a wide range of voices is also an essential part of communication.

Perhaps each of our lists of top schools will include with pride that particular school where we earned our degree. Maybe the ideal theological institution is the one that we view from a distance without seeing any of its blemishes, wishing that we could be on its faculty, student body, staff, or Board of Directors. On the other hand, perhaps the ATS needs to set forth its "ideal seminary"—an all-star cast of superstar faculty, staff, students—then hold up this particular school as the model that all theological institutions are directed to emulate.

## The Search for a Common
## Definition of Excellence

At a faculty forum on our seminary campus, colleagues were articulating the diversity in our own midst. Maybe the top seminaries are those that have satisfactorily worked out a balance between unity and diversity on their campuses. Or does it serve a school better to gravitate intentionally in the direction of unity at the cost of diversity, or toward diversity at the loss of unity? It could well be that the top schools need to look beyond the measurable terms I identified earlier. In the final analysis, is the selection of the top schools a qualitative matter more than a quantitative issue? Or is it something else? Do accrediting agencies ever agree among themselves on measurable standards regarding "the good theological school?"[5]

The best that I can determine is that accrediting agencies in practice want each institution to establish its own goals and mission. We are then encouraged to examine ourselves critically to ascertain to what extent these goals are being implemented and upheld by the institution. The accrediting agency does not impose its own list of the top ten, but it does call for *institutional integrity* from its member schools, meaning that each school ought to live up to the goals and mission it has declared for itself. This is what an institutional Self-Study Report for accreditation review is all about.

Institutional integrity requires that we articulate the foundational grounds for each school. There is more than one model for theological education. Each school's identity must be evaluated within this larger conglomerate of models. For instance, there is the university model of theological education. In this model, the faculty views itself as a graduate school of academia, with strong emphasis on research and publication. The classroom and the library are the two focal points of interest. The faculty in this model does not necessarily ascribe or confess to a common body of theological beliefs. The emphasis is upon the historical, sociological, and philosophical underpinnings behind religious convictions with sensitivity toward the global context and the realities of cultural pluralism. Non-denominational university schools, such as the University of Chicago Divinity School and the Harvard Divinity School, follow this model of instruction.

There is also the monastic model of theological education, which emphasizes spiritual formation while pursuing studies. Most Roman Catholic and Orthodox seminaries emulate this model. Here, the chapel and opportunities for meditation tend to be the primary points of interest rather than the class-room. The thrust is upon developing the spiritual character and priestly skills of the seminarian.

A third model is the denominational (and interdenominational) model of theological education, as witnessed in the Protestant theological seminaries in the ATS (some 118 out of 243 schools). While there is great variety (com-binations of the university and monastic models) within these denominational schools, each essentially reflects from close to loose denominational ties to its ecclesiastical supporters. All of these schools have the tendency to derive their mission for being from the church and not simply from the academic community of higher education. That is to say, the denominational seminary is aware that it is a *graduate school of the church* as much as a graduate school of academia.

Naturally, there is a creative tension inherent in the denominational model. The faculty seeks to pursue the critical study of theology and biblical studies with academic freedom and, yet, is expected to be faithful to the confessional affiliation of the seminary. In other words, denominationally oriented schools require faculty members to be believers who are comfortable with the main tenets of the denomination represented by the school. In this confessional model, the classroom and the chapel are ideally (but not always in practice) held in equal importance  scholarship and piety are seen in partnership within the seminarian's pilgrimage to be a learned spiritual leader.

Excellence in theological education, it seems, is measured according to dif-ferent criteria suitable to each school's foundational goal. Within each of these three basic models, there are inherent values if the school is to be well regarded. From this perspective, perhaps it would be more meaningful to highlight a few well functioning examples within each essential model of theological education rather than to speak in general terms of "the top schools."

## Building Community
## as the Key to Excellence

The deeper question may not be which are the top schools, but rather which are the top theological communities we wish to commend and emulate in our churches. Which schools exemplify a community of spiritual learners where healthy relationships exist? After all, isn't the reality of relationships with God and with one another at the heart of the matter in leading human life to become more human? But how can you measure relationships? There is really no formal course called "Relationship 101" or "Community 101."[6] The fact that twenty-two out of twenty-three of our full-time faculty at Pittsburgh Seminary have an earned doctorate is important to the school's standing, but the more significant factor that contributes to the climate of learning is the actual investment of time each faculty and staff member makes in relationships. *The quality of relationships on campus is the most outstanding factor that makes any school "tops" for the students who go there.* We need a more student-sensitive rather than faculty-centered assessment in evaluating the educational quality of life in our theological schools.[7]

Whenever campus politics polarize faculty and students, community life is diminished. It is far healthier for a campus to have several issues under discussion rather than to be polarized by a single issue, preventing a wider web of communication to continue on and off campus. Communication involves listening as well as sharing, but above all, communication requires a common desire for truth-telling, beginning with each person. Trust is built upon truth, and healthy relationships depend on relating that truth in moments of forgiving love among ourselves. Avoiding the pain of truth contributes to superficial relationships and hollowness in our life together.

The beautiful thing to witness on any seminary or divinity school campus is the process of truth-telling taking place among colleagues and students. It is my guess that there isn't a theological campus that isn't yearning to become a better community where freedom and forgiveness prevail. No one can take truth-telling for granted; we need to work on it constantly. Our campuses can be deceptive; communication sometimes gets distorted by misplaced piety and compassion. It has been my observation that the prevailing culture (whether it be conservative, liberal, or moderate) on many theological campuses neglects the tough side of truth-telling; rather, we often seem to be more comfortable with simply being nice to one another. Unfortunately, as someone has observed, "Nice only gets you a C+ in life." Maybe this situation is no different in other organizations; the moment of truth for some doesn't begin until an economic recession requires changes, while theological institutions that enjoy financial stability are sometimes tempted to neglect their responsibility for truth-telling.

*The difference between excellence and mediocrity reduces itself ultimately to the common resolve in each institution to be a committed, disciplined, and truthful community.* In an academic institution of shared governance, blame as well as success is a collective matter. If a "top ten" list is published tomorrow and your institution is not among the ten, who are you going to blame? Ownership of both blame and success belongs to us all. We are all stakeholders when it comes to our theological schools—including our churches and demanding critics.

The challenge confronting theological educators today is to establish basic criteria for excellence and then to have the intestinal fortitude to back these standards. Only then will theological education further its scholarly and spiritual influence among churches and throughout society.

Basic criteria in any evaluative process for excellence might include: 1) academic competence, 2) spiritual vitality, 3) financial soundness, 4) healthy relationships, 5) committed trustees, and 6) graduates' professional performance and fulfillment. These six criteria are interrelated and interdependent. Together, they direct us toward becoming a community of sojourners who care enough to always seek improvement, speaking the truth in love and forgiving one another.

Rationalizations, and even legitimate excuses, for our failures will not produce results. In the future, we will need to be tougher on ourselves if theological education is to forge greater advances in the church and society. To be counted among the top theological schools must be a goal; to publish a list of the "top ten" is of secondary importance. Our primary attention must center on commitment, discipline, and truth in our theological communities, as we establish a defensible standard of excellence expected of all institutions in higher education, including seminaries and divinity schools.

### DISCUSSION STARTER

*I*n addition to the importance of having healthy relationships on campus, we could add the following noteworthy characteristics that ought to be found among top schools:

1. a curriculum that allows space for critical reflection with opportunities for the integration of academic and field-based experiences;
2. an ethos that supports a dual emphasis on academic and spiritual formation, thus uniting scholarship and piety for everyone in the learning community;
3. an emphasis on leadership development and acceptance of diversity;
4. faculty who lead in exemplifying a commitment to scholarship and piety;
5. faculty who take time to mentor students and are accessible;
6. faculty who are learners as well as teachers and students who are teachers as well as learners;
7. the practice of wise stewardship of financial resources in fulfilling its mission;
8. flexibility within a school's mission to address unexpected learning circumstances;

9. knowledge of how to adapt well to change in a post-Gutenberg (digital) era;
10. knowledge of the institution's culture and tradition when conversing with the wider interfaith community;
11. support for global-oriented programs that address:
    a. evangelism,
    b. ecumenical relations,
    c. interfaith cooperation,
    d. peace and justice, and
    e. global and local links.

What would you add to or subtract from the above list of characteristics in drawing your profile of the top theological school? Do you view your own theological school as being static or is it a work in progress towards excellence? What are you doing to help your school to advance in its ranking in addition to being a good teacher, good student, good trustee, etc.?

Chapter 3

# Academic Freedom and Seminary Education

*T*wo interlocking values *must* steer theological education: academic freedom and academic excellence. These two values must be present while schools discuss their long-range plans, theological disputes, faculty replacements, facility upgrades, campus safety, chapel services, enrollment needs, and the constant demand for added financial resources. Academic freedom is necessary if academic excellence is our educational goal. Any lesser goal would indeed reduce the credibility and contribution of theological education in society.

Seminaries, as graduate schools, need to focus on the challenge of academic freedom, however, as graduate schools of the church, most theological schools also have a confessional faith context with ecclesiastical loyalties. Herein lies their tension: Can seminaries truly practice academic freedom as a confessionally defined religious institution of higher education and achieve academic excellence? Do academic freedom and excellence in seminaries differ qualitatively from freedom and excellence in secular universities?

### Does Tenure Enhance
### Academic Freedom and Excellence?

The biblical understanding of freedom actually liberates religious institutions of higher education, including theological schools, to pursue truth wherever it leads. We believe that God frees us to seek truth and not fear it. Yet, how free do my colleagues feel as we carry out our teaching, writing, and research duties at the seminary?

Academic freedom seems to have deteriorated in the halls of theological education today. I'm not thinking simply of the fundamentalist takeover of Southern Baptist seminaries and the apparent resulting curtailment of academic freedom. It seems to me that rigorous academic scholarship among theological schools today in general is lacking. Some academicians believe that serious religious scholarship has shifted now to universities and colleges through their departments of religious studies. However, it has been my observation that since the Vietnam period, all of higher education, including theological schools, is preoccupied with matters of political and orthodox correctness on our respective campuses. Such a climate tends to dilute rigorous academic scholarship and discussion, especially among younger scholars who are careful not to jeopardize their tenure (or contractual) advancement. Younger scholars sometimes practice a selective silence where their active imput would enhance academic discourse.

Within this apparent caution, the question can seriously be raised, how necessary is tenure for the integrity and freedom of academia? To what extent does academic creativity require tenure? Academic guilds on the whole tend to be conservative, which is evident when accepted norms and implicit self-interests are challenged. Such attitudes thwart the intended spirit of academic freedom and make it difficult for institutions of higher education to break new ground that would advance the self-understanding of culture, church, and society.

Is it possible that we are substituting ideological commitments for balanced investigation and discussion? Many would like to see a seminary as both an educating institution and a "school of the prophets" with the obligation to speak out on matters of contemporary relevance and controversy in a responsible way; we expect our graduates to do the same in their ministries. Unfortunately, since the politicizing of educational institutions (including seminaries) in the 1960s, there are still faculty, students, administrators, and trustees who resent the full burden of academic freedom and who choose to remain silent when they ought to speak up.

Not only is academic freedom not sufficiently exercised in academia, but this situation may even be quietly encouraged by financial backers to the institution who expect (rightly or wrongly) to hear their convictions and beliefs upheld. They question whether they should give financial support to an educational institution that doesn't espouse their personal values and beliefs. I have heard that sentiment more than once from potential donors. When this kind of climate prevails for an educational institution, ideological consideration replaces the pursuit of truth. Faculty, students, and administrators are no longer free, even though they may be well compensated and the students provided with adequate scholarships. True academic investigation cannot take place within inflexible boundaries.

As the discussion has thus far indicated, I am a firm believer in responsible academic freedom and would like to see more evidence of it in the halls of academia. It is also my growing conviction that the existence of tenure for faculty is intended to buttress academic freedom and to enable the institution to maintain academic excellence. Academic freedom with tenure provides a supportive base for faculty when challenging existing assumptions and seeking an extension to frontiers of knowledge. This is especially so if one is not in agreement with what is regarded as "politically or doctrinally correct" at the time. The principle of academic freedom with tenure places emphasis not so much on truth per se, but rather on freedom to *seek the truth*. Those of us in theological education can understand this emphasis, since we know that our own theologizing is not synonymous with divine revelation; the last word on truth belongs to God.

Our seminary, like many colleges and universities across the country, adheres to the "1940 Statement of Principles on Academic Freedom and Tenure," outlined by the American Association of University Professors (AAUP). The standards of the ATS largely echo the AAUP principles, which have undergone subsequent revisions, but maintain their basic advocacy for academic freedom and "responsible liberty of conscience."[1] To protect academic freedom, the AAUP has instituted a process of review that protects the rights of permanent full-time faculty with tenure. Tenure, however, does not imply that a faculty person cannot be dismissed for reasons of just cause, moral turpitude, or financial exigency. Rather, tenure assures that a fair and equitable process of review will be guaranteed and enforced. In academia, the process of review is of paramount importance. If the process is approved by all parties, the outcome is more likely to be accepted.

In practice, tenure tends to be viewed by faculty, administrators, and trustees as job security unless the economic roof collapses on the institution, in which case even tenure is precarious.[2] Most faculty dismissals are due to matters of financial exigency; it is more difficult to defend dismissal for reasons of just cause and moral turpitude as mentioned in the AAUP guidelines. Later in this chapter the importance of establishing and implementing a post-tenure review process for faculty development and institutional vitality will be discussed.

## Confessionalism and Academic Freedom in Seminaries

The problem of academic freedom that theological schools face today is often more subtle. The faculties in most theological institutions are neither fanatics nor fundamentalists; our problem is how to struggle with the meaning of academic freedom within a confessional context. For instance, it is not our practice to invite persons to join the faculty at our seminary who don't believe in God; in fact we ask our full-time faculty to sign the official registry of the seminary and thereby witness before the Board of Directors their confession of

faith in God. We ask the same of our trustee-directors. It is within this confessional context that we struggle with our understanding of academic freedom, even though we are aware that we can also learn from atheists and
heretics. We must always be clear on our commitment to openness; believers
need have no fear in their pursuit of truth.

Is academic freedom different then for Pittsburgh Seminary than, for
instance, the neighboring University of Pittsburgh and Carnegie Mellon University? Listen to this statement approved by our faculty, administration, and
Board, in the bylaws of our school:

> The Seminary supports the policy of academic tenure. While the Seminary
> is proud to be identified with the Reformed tradition embodied in the Pres-
> byterian Church, it desires nevertheless to maintain an interdependent rela-
> tionship with the church. The emphasis is upon interdependence, not
> dependency, lest the Seminary forfeit the demands of free inquiry required
> of an institution of learning in carrying out its task. Academic freedom,
> however, within the context of a faith commitment characteristic of a theo-
> logical school and her tradition does have a built-in tension that must be rec-
> ognized and addressed in each ad hoc situation.[3]

In other words, the quality of academic freedom and excellence pursued in
our seminary has an added burden not carried by the faculties of universities.
A confessional requirement is not asked of university faculty members. Atheists as well as believers can serve on their faculties. This is not the case for
theological institutions. There is the clear expectation that the leadership and
faculty of our school will be believers who are comfortable with the convictions of the Reformed heritage.

Therefore, for us there is the extra responsibility to pursue academic
excellence in the context of this self-limiting understanding of academic
freedom. *Learning for us is done in the context of our faith with the strong
commitment that the journey of faith is also a journey for truth.* Ultimately,
we do not believe there is a contradiction. We believe that faith and the pursuit of truth are complementary emphases that support each other. This, of
course, is the scholarly premise on which we operate. We believe there is an
integrated and symbiotic interplay between the seminary chapel and the
classroom that sets us apart from other graduate schools, even though the
academic standards at the seminary and at universities are not that different
in essence and we are all subject to similar accrediting agencies and their
requirements.

In 1997, the AAUP sponsored a conference on Academic Freedom at Religiously Affiliated Institutions that recognized the issue of academic freedom
in higher education as a common concern at theological schools, as well as

colleges and universities. Jonathan Alger, AAUP counsel and organizer of the conference, summed up the observations of the participants:

> Disputes over the extent to which religious dogma should restrict expression or inquiry at church-related institutions are partly an outgrowth of larger debates about the public role of religion in society. In recent years, forces outside the academy have played an increasingly prominent role in reassessing the ecclesiastical content of church-related institutions—a development that parallels in some ways the outside political pressures and corporate models that have prompted a re-examination of other aspects of higher education (such as the tenure system) from a non-academic perspective. These forces remind us that with or without a religious affiliation, colleges and universities are not completely autonomous but part of a larger community with constituencies pursuing agendas that may be at odds with the unfettered pursuit of academic freedom.[4]

Maintaining academic freedom will always be a constant struggle in the academy, and theological schools are not exempt from that struggle. However, we should not tolerate any form of academic freedom with tenure that understands itself solely as job security. Instead, we should be supportive of academic freedom with tenure when it challenges us to broaden our horizons, to question academic "conclusions," or to be critical of status quo practices within the church and society.

Theological institutions are committed to educating women and men for ministry in its many forms, by understanding our past in order to appreciate the present situation, by envisioning the future, and by advancing the body of knowledge through responsible investigation, faithfully discharging our duties before God who values our freedom. The theological scholar is driven by the conviction that in the final analysis there is neither tension between academic freedom and belief, nor between belief and academic excellence. Seminaries ought to understand well the integral bond between academic freedom and excellence in their pursuit and witness to the truth.

## Guidelines for the Future

The best means of assuring both freedom and excellence in graduate theological education is tenure. It would therefore be prudent for administrators, trustees, and faculty of our institutions to consider the following four guidelines within the context of tenure.

1. Academic standards, institutional needs, and strategic priorities must be clearly articulated and periodically reviewed by each school, independent of actual tenure-granting situations. Personal sentiments toward tenure candidates

and turf issues oftentimes confuse objective consideration to the detriment of the institution's interest and the lives of personnel and students served by the school. Faculty, administrators, and trustees must aim for a stability that is responsive to the realities of change. Institutions need to manage well the pressures for continuity and the demands for change.

2. Faculty, administrators, and trustees must not equate tenure with lifetime employment. For the sake of the institution and the credibility of tenured professors, a rigorously and regularly enforced process of post-tenure evaluation must be established. The administration and faculty review committee should appoint one or two consultants to assist in the evaluating process to assure objectivity. Other evaluative tools should also be developed such as questionnaires for students, graduates, and colleagues—careful consideration should be given not only to publication and teaching, but also to new course development, collegiality, and contributions to campus life on behalf of students as well as to the church and civic community.

It is in everyone's best interest to improve the post-tenure evaluative process for the sake of the institution's credibility before peers and students. This is not an easy process; it seems faculty shy away from judging their peers or themselves. Post-tenure reviews, however, are a constructive means of faculty development.[5] Such reviews might reveal methods to enhance teaching through technology with a resulting faculty development fund to make this possible. Frustration with research and publication efforts may lead through honest collegiality to fresh angles of approach. Post-tenure faculty reviews will help faculty members to be frank with themselves. The aim of all peer reviews is to support colleagues for their own sake and to enhance the school as a learning community. Theological schools cannot afford public perceptions that we are unproductive and receiving a "free ride." Financial support is attracted to an exciting learning community that brings educational value to the church and community.

3. Alternative approaches to tenure such as extended contracts have advantages and disadvantages. A contractual approach may provide flexibility, especially for financially weaker institutions. However, such a policy also tends to diminish institutional loyalty and freedom of expression.[6] Perhaps instead we ought to consider supporting a limited core of tenured faculty supplemented by regular part-time faculty. The latter group would enjoy more than an adjunct status. Part-time faculty would primarily consist of practitioners who have distinguished themselves in the field or in their area of expertise. This is a practice already utilized by medical and law schools. It can become a means by which theological schools could enjoy the best of both worlds, namely, the stability provided by a core tenured faculty and the pres-

ence of a regular part-time faculty to assure flexibility and attention to special needs. Such a working format would also be in keeping with the ATS standards for accreditation, where the following is stated regarding the faculty:

> Although accredited institutions are not required to adopt tenure as an appointment policy, it is expected that there will be such institutional conditions and procedures as will sustain in an orderly fashion a body of scholars and teachers with reasonable assurance of continuity and sufficient duration of appointment and academic freedom as to engender both commitment and stability.[7]

4. In addition to our advocacy of academic freedom and excellence, trustees and tenured faculty must also recognize the need for finding other means of expressing our approval and acceptance of younger scholars and gifted administrators who also contribute significantly within our theological schools. Since junior faculty and administrators do not normally have tenure, their level of frustration and anxiety tends to be higher than tenured colleagues. Much of this, I feel, is unfortunate. It creates an unnecessary hierarchy within the learning community. It is time we acknowledge to ourselves that the bestowing of tenure is essentially a psychological rite of passage—a way of expressing institutional affirmation and acceptance. Shouldn't we find other suitable means in addition to tenure to express approval and acceptance for the important contributions that untenured scholars and administrators also make in our midst? What we need to avoid, and what is too often found, is the pervasive feeling among junior faculty, administrators, and part-time instructors that they are non-persons in their institutions because they are without tenure. As I suggested earlier, some fail to exercise their "academic freedom" for fear that established tenured faculty will disapprove of their comments. Whether this is true or merely their perception, it is certainly detrimental to the welfare of the whole institution. *It takes more than a core of tenured faculty members to enable a school to fulfill its mission.*

An educational institution is far more complex than many of us are willing to acknowledge. Most theological schools haven't personnel to spare. In actuality, everyone in the institution is responsible for upholding the values of freedom and excellence. We are made aware of this reality when we encourage among ourselves an atmosphere of mutual acceptance and respect. Furthermore, tenure should not be a barrier to faculty teamwork; trust is needed among all colleagues, tenured and non-tenured, if the institution is to advance its mission. Working together, we must strive for excellence and freedom for theological schools within the graduate community of higher education.

## DISCUSSION STARTER

*H*as this chapter influenced you to change any biases that you may have brought to the subject of tenure and its relation to academic freedom and excellence? Unfortunately, our own self-interests and institutional interests tend to throw more heat than light on this subject. It is truly difficult to be "objective" on the subject of tenure.

As one who holds a dual appointment as Professor of Theology (a tenured position) and President of the Seminary (a non-tenured position), I can see the advantages and disadvantages of tenure in relation to academic freedom and upholding institutional excellence. Frankly, I oscillate on the subject when I witness tenure being undermined by academics who fail to live up to their commitments while expecting the institution's commitment to them to remain steadfast. Such practices weaken the respect for tenure and should be more vigorously questioned by the tenured faculty. At the same time, I see no worthy alternative to tenure that promises a measure of support for both the institution and the faculty. Each approach has its trade-offs. Every theological school needs to make its own determination as to what is the wisest policy for its situation in the context of a market-driven economy where few guarantees, if any, exist for either individuals or institutions. Flexibility is the desired goal of operation.

As a faculty member, I certainly want to keep my options open so that I can pursue my love for teaching, research, and reflection with freedom, which encourages me to remain with the institution that supports me in these endeavors. As a seminary president, I also want the institution's options to be open, for the sake of the school's continued viability, which calls for constant adaptation in our services to churches and communities. Yet the financial and campus realities as well as student demographics place us at times in a "catch-22" situation in which the options for either party are terribly limited. Whatever the case, the institution needs to commit itself by whatever system is chosen—tenure or non-tenure—to uphold a fair process of evaluation that is clearly spelled out to all interested parties.

Those who believe that the tenure system stands in the way of seminary renewal will discover, if they haven't already, that the absence of tenure is not a panacea for renewal either. Institutional renewal does not depend solely on the issue of tenure. To think so would lead to a misplaced debate when the more serious consideration before us is whether the mission or purpose of the institution is being successfully fulfilled. The appropriateness of tenure or its substitute must be seen then in light of the school's critical review of its mission for the future. What do you think?

Chapter 4

# Who Owns the Seminary?

$A$ fourth challenge facing theological institutions is to clarify the interdependent relationship among the stakeholders of theological education. Without a clear grasp of this interdependence so necessary for the advancement of the theological enterprise, we will undermine ourselves before a general public that is already largely ignorant or indifferent to our presence.[1] In other words, a more viable partnership among the stakeholders of theological education than presently exists is urgently needed. Today, this issue along with those already discussed in the previous chapters such as 1) the leadership crisis among the churches, 2) the misdirected competition for excellence among theological schools, and 3) the false expectations and frustrations surrounding academic freedom, are actually all related parts of a seamless tapestry of challenges confronting theological education. These challenges by no means exhaust the list of issues before theological schools and supporters.

## The Issue of Accountability

Having now spent nearly four decades in the employment of seminaries, I have asked myself more than once, "What drives a seminary?" Who claims ownership over the theological enterprise of educating today's and tomorrow's leaders? Who are the stakeholders? Who is in charge? Who claims accountability? Is it the faculty? They are certainly the heart of the institution. Is it the Board of Directors? They hold the ultimate legal and fiduciary responsibilities for the institution and set policy. Is it the student body? We wouldn't have much of a seminary without the enthusiasm and stimulating questions raised by students. Is it the alumni/alumnae? The seminary cannot move forward without listening to the voices of its graduates.

What, then, drives the seminary? Is it the administration, with the hard work and faithfulness of the staff? If the faculty is the heart of the institution, perhaps the secretaries, custodians, maintenance workers, and administration are its soul. Is it the professional guilds that faculty associate with that drive the seminary? Peer loyalty is a significant factor. Is it the accreditation process that ascertains whether we are attaining the norms expected of a fully bona fide institution? Every school has a desire to match and surpass the standards of accreditation that enhance the school's standing.

Have we yet found a satisfactory answer to what drives the seminary? Is it the latest concerns at the grassroots such as evangelism, peacemaking, justice issues, the environment, etc. that drive the seminary? Certainly, the agenda presented to the seminary has short- and long-range implications and needs to be sorted out. Is it the curriculum? There is constant debate concerning the subject matter taught in a seminary. Or is it the seminary's purpose and mission statement? The school's self-understanding and historic ethos are certainly on the list enabling a theological school to stay focused on its goal.

Recently, two visitors on our campus were representing our national denomination in studying theological institutions of our church. They questioned trustees, faculty, and administration as to whether the school has a clear sense of vision and identity. The responses they heard, I suspect, were both yes and no. "Yes," we have a statement of purpose in our catalog as to what we are about, but "no," we are not always clear on the strategies and ways to fulfill our mission in the context of constant change.

As we look back on the history of our schools, we need regularly to examine and revise, as well as reaffirm our statement of purpose as a living, dynamic institution. In light of our purpose and changing needs, we need to evaluate our current curriculum; we must also look at our present composition of faculty and envision what we would like our future service to be. Who is accountable as we plan our future?

Realistically, we know that we can only get from here to there by planning step by step. Hence, all interested constituents of the seminary—trustees, faculty, students, alumni/ae, administrators, and other stakeholders—must review the numerous requests made of us and revise our dreams in the light of our mission statement. Hopefully, there will be in all quarters of the seminary's extended community a lively discussion of our purpose. Through a process of renewed vigor we can gain a new sense of ownership over our theological enterprise in our quest to be the ideal seminary. But will all of our combined efforts be sufficient for reaching our goal?

## God Drives the Seminary

What drives a seminary goes beyond its mission statement. It is centered in the power of God's Spirit that ignites and persuades us to move ahead in faith.

Our belief that there is a future with God is what motivates us to give ourselves to God, thereby transforming our lives and communities.

What ultimately drives the seminary is a conscious dependence upon the Spirit of the living God within our learning communities. When all is said and done, the main driving force in seminaries is this living presence of God, who is the major Stakeholder and Provider of theological wisdom, who is assumed but unfortunately neglected in the course of our educational process as we demystify the sacred materials of faith. Nevertheless, as David Kelsey insists, we must not lose sight of the fact that the role of theological education is committed "to understand[ing] God truly."[2]

What finally ought to drive all interested parties (stakeholders) is this vision to enhance our faith and trust in God and to communicate the theological wisdom gained through our educational experiences for the benefit of all. Unfortunately, however, it has been my observation that oftentimes those of us who claim we trust in God are the most insecure and have not incarnated within our hearts, minds, and souls what we proclaim, teach, and study. This may be why the simple faith of a child or the trust in God found among suffering people touches our emotions and preempts our academic learning, informing us in the midst of our sophistication and earned degrees that we truly know nothing without the divine gifts of grace and wisdom. This is the vision of theologizing practiced in the (Eastern) Orthodox tradition and ecumenically by Christian mystics. It reminds us of the fact that theological wisdom is above all a gift given to the learned and unlearned by the grace of God. Realizing once again that we are all recipients of God's grace should especially humble those of us who are theological educators. The reality is that the academic degrees earned by us and issued through our schools do not necessarily guarantee that our faith has grown. Yet, isn't this what theological education in its totality seeks to achieve—the deepening of one's faith through the study of theological wisdom? (Matthew 22:36-40). This is a paradox that faces all of us who are engaged in theological education. We operate our schools, teach, write our books, and seek accreditation as if it all depends on us, the stakeholders, when in reality it all depends on the Spirit of God who imparts divine wisdom that empowers us to fulfill our destiny and equips us with a message of hope for a society in search of its soul.

How we relate and balance these interests is vitally important if our schools are to fulfill their mission. Trustees must not only be mindful of the important stakeholders and driving forces behind the support of theological schools, but also be aware of the collective and interdependent responsibilities these stakeholders have when asked the question, "Who owns the seminary?"

At the center of these stakeholders is the Chief Stakeholder who is God alone, the foundational ground for all our stakeholders. As we seek to love God more truly, the divine presence gives vitality to our schools, whereas the divine absence spells death no matter how large our endowment. We need to confess openly and regularly (through our worship together) this transcendent foundation for our existence as we navigate through our conflicts, unifying stakeholders in the collective creativity of seminary life with its excitement, tears, and rewards.

## Should Society Listen to and Support Seminaries?

But what if theological schools disappeared tomorrow; would it make any difference? What does theological education actually contribute to society? Do seminaries have a public role in addition to their ecclesiastical responsibilities to churches and religious causes?

These questions were raised at a consultation held at ATS headquarters recently. Our task force was asked to brainstorm with the ATS staff in drafting a case for corporate business and community support of theological education. Why should business, and the public at large, support theological schools? Can seminaries serve sectarian and non-sectarian purposes at the same time? Is anyone in the community really listening to us?[3] After all, isn't the primary mission of seminaries to serve churches and related religious institutions by graduating informed and committed leadership? Should we expect more than this from seminaries? The answer is yes.

In addition to preparing leaders for ecclesiastical organizations, seminaries also offer invaluable service to secular society: We nurture and support the community's sense of hope for itself. Without hope, society loses its direction, purpose, and motivation to excel. Having hope motivates and advances a society's sense of well-being.

Of course, societies can be organized around other qualities as well. More often than not, we organize around tribal mentalities and act accordingly. This unfortunate approach sets us up to be divided along ethnic, racial, gender, and class boundaries. We organize ourselves against one another; we see this happening nationally and around the world. Bosnia isn't the only place where those who hate together stay together.

The ultimate aim of theological education is to indicate that there is a better way to organize and humanize ourselves. But is the surrounding society receiving this message from us? The design of any theological school's curriculum is to provide a foundation that inspires hope—a hope that is neither utopian nor narrowly conceived to exclude others. Seminaries and divinity schools recognize that the subject of hope undergoes numerous interpretations reflecting a wide range of religious traditions. Nevertheless, theological schools highlight the importance of hope—a necessary factor if our society is to survive in good health.

The capacity to hope is essential to our humanity; to try to live without it is hell. Hope enables us to face the worst of circumstances, igniting the spirit of innovation within us as we explore creative solutions. Hope helps us to transcend the tendency to be greedy and violent. Without hope, we rob ourselves of enthusiasm and an adventurous spirit. To trade off the future for immediate gratification as some are doing will cheat us of our inheritance.

As critical centers of learning, seminaries teach hope without ignoring the economic, social, political, and psychological realities that reflect the complexity of modern society within today's global context. Theological education provides another vantage point from which to understand the human condition. To this end, for instance, our seminary established some years ago an Institute for Metro-Urban Ministry and a Center on Business, Religion, and Public Life. We seek through these means to address difficult urban concerns with a sense of hope rather than despair within our business-oriented culture. We also have possibilities for joint degree programs with the three universities in Pittsburgh in the fields of social work, urban ministry and management, music, law, and information and library science. Other theological schools have similar joint degree opportunities and certification programs. We believe these academic and non-academic programs within our theological schools can benefit a broad cross-section of our society, also encouraging business and professional organizations to support our schools in their goal to serve churches and communities more relevantly.

However, in spite of such modest social and educational efforts, increasing numbers of American citizens are giving up; the pursuit of happiness and a fulfilling life seem to be beyond their grasp. We are becoming, it seems, a society driven by despair rather than hope, even in the midst of our affluence.[4] With the loss of hope, we are becoming disillusioned, confused, and less human with one another. The high crime rate is but one indication of this. The "cold war" of yesterday is now the "hot war" of shootings at home. Building more prisons, warehouses of human flesh, isn't the solution to this loss of hope for victims or for inmates. Frankly, it takes more than money to build a better society. We also need to come to terms with the significant loss of hope within us. Neither rich nor poor are exempt from these feelings. Indeed, we face a value crisis today—what many in an earlier era called a "spiritual crisis." At the heart of this crisis is our loss of hope.

Theological centers of learning do not have a monopoly on instilling hope in society; but our schools are committed to faith in God as the ultimate hope. Seminaries and divinity schools provide a learned and realistic framework in which to evaluate various models of hope in the public arena. Critical theological study liberates us from false hopes and fundamentalist ideologies, whether secular or religious in their origin. Hope in God enables us to face every kind of circumstance, while aiming for a more humane society. Biblically inspired hope looks forward to the kingdom of God—where peace, justice, and equality prevail. This vision of the kingdom of God is basic to the believer's understanding of hope; religious traditions take their bearings around this core understanding of hope.

If theological schools should disappear tomorrow, not only would churches and religiously related institutions be impoverished, but society would also miss these learning centers of hope that humanize and motivate us to be nobler than we are, as we acknowledge with humility—our ultimate accountability before God. Isn't this what is implied when as a society we claim, "In God We Trust"? While we who are called to the theological enterprise wish to encourage society to listen to us and support our best practices, we in turn need to make a more concerted effort to include the larger public and communities where we are situated as stakeholders in the theological enterprise that engages us.

### DISCUSSION STARTER

*O*wnership of our theological schools entails a far wider circle of inclusion than we normally recognize in practice. Ownership of our schools starts with God and ends with society, and within this range of ownership there is more interdependence than we have admitted to ourselves.

Adding the number of stakeholders to the theological enterprise further complicates what is already a complex matrix, making it difficult to provide a simple answer to the question, "Who owns the seminary?" Should the voices of trustees, students, faculty, and graduates be weighted more heavily than those from donors, foundation executives, and accrediting agencies? What emphasis should be placed on the concerns and complaints from the pews and pulpits in seminary matters? How responsive should we be to the thoughtful comments of those who might be regarded as "church dropouts" and critics? What weight should be given to denominational officials and neighborhood leaders who may not necessarily share your school's particular faith orientation or direction?

How willing are we to engage with the wider circle of voices off campus in our decision-making process? To what extent should we restrict the widening of our public until we first resolve within our learning communities the question as to whether we are sufficiently sensitive to students in structuring our curriculum and the content of our academic programs? Behind all these voices is the looming issue of ownership and governance. Furthermore, how connected to or dependent on churches and communities do theological schools wish to be? To what extent are theological educators willing to change their agenda in order to address larger community expectations? In other words, do all the stakeholders share a common agenda? Whom have we left out? And should all interested parties have voice and vote if we want to move beyond a "clerical paradigm" for theological education?

# PART II  Program Challenges

Chapter 5

# Tomorrow's Seminary Curriculum

*I*nstituting a creatively integrated curriculum based on *forgiving*, I submit, is a significant way to restore theological coherence within our historic fourfold seminary disciplines—Bible, theology, church history, and practical theology. With such a focus, tomorrow's curriculum would strengthen and nurture us to become disciples of forgiveness for a fragmented world. By this means, theological education could make a greater contribution to our comprehensive understanding of forgiveness, while equipping and empowering the people of God to be reconcilers in our interdependent and broken world.

Edward Farley, who taught for many years at Vanderbilt University Divinity School, devoted a great deal of his intellectual efforts toward the reform of theological education. Unfortunately, the fragmentation of theological education that concerned Farley continues.[1] The status quo is largely in place in theological schools even though faculties and student bodies have become more diverse than a decade ago. In a recent interview, Farley said, "I am a little pessimistic because faculty members come out of graduate schools with a loyalty to a particular field and it is very hard to get their attention or arouse their passion for larger sets of problems, such as pedagogy or the reform of theological education . . . . Therefore, it is very hard to get seminaries to really change what they do."[2]

Farley also observes that the "clerical paradigm" that has long ruled reinforces the existing curriculum so that theological education is seen as simply clergy education. "When it dominates a school, the theological student is seen as a future 'professional' who must learn 'theory' to be applied to 'practice.' This isolates theological wisdom into 'academic disciplines,' which then seem irrelevant and empties practice (what ministers do as ministers) of theological understanding."[3] This condition ought to motivate us to review the curriculum in theological schools from the standpoint of ministry by the people of God (clergy and laity in partnership together), ministry no longer limited to a "clerical paradigm." We need to work together as God's people to plan a program of theological study that will enable us to articulate an effective witness wherever the highways of learning lead us.[4]

A college student who was visiting our campus appeared at my office door recently and asked simply, "*What* do you learn in seminary?" Well, of course, I could answer that we master Hebrew and Greek, analyze the Bible and theological dogmatics from cover to cover, become prophets in the pulpit, and finely hone our counseling skills! However, our conversation covered a more basic range of subjects. The student noted that various graduate schools are easily categorized by their intended mission—for instance, a medical school is associated with healing and acquiring diagnostic skills; a law school is interested in interpreting regulations and the rights of citizens within due process; business schools are concerned with profit-making and management; and an engineering school with precision calculations and projects. But what is the main thrust of the theological school?

Seminary education, I explained, is dedicated to interpreting and integrating biblically informed faith to human experience. The task of the theological school specifically is to educate and develop learned leadership among the people of God, the Body of Christ. The effectiveness of the seminary's efforts can be measured by how graduates sustain and satisfy a congregation of believers and inquirers in their quest for truth and fulfillment, overwhelmed at times by the presence of violence, suspicion, injustice, and lack of direction. Neither our younger nor older seminarians are interested in being simply keepers of the institutional church. Most seminarians are eager to transform society and to breathe new life into the organizational church. The unspoken question for all seminary educators is whether we are aiding or impeding these seminarians in accomplishing their goals.

We are keenly aware that religious institutions have declined in membership over the past several decades, but many of us recognize new stirrings; there is certainly a great deal of interest in "grassroots spirituality" within and outside the life of the church. Surveys, if they are to be believed, inform us that three out of every five Americans continue to support religion-related institutions, and two out of five Americans participate regularly in worship services. Over 90 percent of our population claim they believe in God whether they go to church or not. In spite of the decline of clergy influence in our society, the pastor in many communities is still an important voice and an opinion maker whose advice is sought. In short, religion is certainly not dead in American life. Clergy are still interpreters of religion at the grassroots level, and this factor brings us to the basic purpose of the seminary. How does the seminary adequately prepare future pastors to be responsible interpreters of the faith? What is central to all our interpretations at the seminary? What message do we want to instill in our graduates as they take up their respective ministries? What is the authentic measurement of true faith? Or is there any measurement at all?

Most theological educators self-consciously reflect on their task; this process of critical reflection helps them to be interpreters of the faith. The seminary is basically a hermeneutical institute fashioned around a traditional fourfold curricular structure that focuses on the disciplines of Bible, theology, church history, and practical theology. Variations and sub-specialties are built around this basic fourfold structure which is often referred to as a "theological encyclopedia."[5]

## Theological Education without a Central Focus

Farley charges that seminary education under this fourfold paradigm has no theological coherence. No common theological understanding exists among the various disciplines of a seminary faculty, and a common end or purpose to unify theological education is missing today. A plurality of agenda and minimal dialogue comprise the seminary environment. Like many congregations, seminary faculties are polite, congenial, and seek to avoid conflict; thus most faculty members tend to work in isolation from one another. Farley makes a plea for dialogue and theological coherence, but does not suggest what the content of this theological unity might be. Identifying this unity is a task for those in every seminary community to ponder, discuss, and debate among themselves and in consultation with the church. Such an exercise can be healthy for a seminary seeking a clearer identity as a graduate professional school and as a graduate school of the church.

Actually, the question, "What do we learn in seminary?" finds its answer through the curriculum. Developing a curriculum is primarily a responsibility of the faculty, but we should also desire input from those in the pews who are interested in theological education. To reflect on this need for wider input and ownership in the curriculum process, many seminaries now require their boards of directors as trustees to have final ownership by reviewing and approving major revisions within the curriculum. Perhaps the faculty needs to initiate an even larger circle of feedback with all the stakeholders of theological education as discussed in the previous chapter. The aim of the curriculum is to graduate learned and committed leaders who can apply the acquired knowledge and skills within their neighborhoods where needed. However, we cannot presuppose that this transition from the classroom to the parish is taking place. In fact, specialization within the seminary faculty can contribute to incoherence if students are unable to synthesize a core message from the many separate voices speaking through the curriculum.

Farley argues that as long as faculty members defend their respective specializations, genuine reform for all practical purposes is next to impossible.[6] For Farley, the big question is: Are faculty willing to contribute to and participate in the academic program holistically to a greater extent than is thus far evident? Is there openness to change in how we carry on the business of educating in our theological schools? Are most revisions of curriculum simply cosmetic dressing around the status quo that fail to harmonize our voices into a shared message? To what extent is theological education sensitive to the stresses and confusion found in local churches? And to what extent is the confusion at local churches due to the lack of coherence in our curriculum? Is the curriculum in our schools simply a projection of faculty interests and needs? What overriding bias is there among theological faculties today— to what degree are we controlled by old wineskins and when do we begin to stitch new ones? Seminary communities should not be considered safe havens from the turmoil and confusion felt at the grassroots; seminaries and churches are connected institutions that need to support one another in articulating the gospel in a changing society.

Unfortunately, there continues to be a gap today between learning and doing in seminary life.[7] Both are essential, but seminarians often tend to be involved too deeply in ministry before proper study has taken place, subjecting them to charges of ministerial malpractice. This is a constant dilemma faced both by seminarians and by church officials who desire their services. Students need early involvement in ministry but not without structured guidance and times for reflection. A seminary is more than a training or "how to" school; it is primarily a theological academy of interpretation on behalf of the church's mission to proclaim the gospel. Constant vigilance, study, spiritual accountability, and discipline are required within the seminaries and the structure of each ecclesial tradition to enhance the ministry of the people of God.

Furthermore, to have learned clergy and laity dependent upon a theological faculty is not enough. We also need a unifying purpose to join intellect and piety in partnership. We need to recover a common theological base for both action and reflection as believers. The college student who stopped in my office was really asking me a fundamental question when inquiring "What do you learn in seminary?" To me the student's question meant, how does theological education make human life more human? What unique knowledge and skills are acquired from the seminary that can address the dehumanizing forces and temptations of the marketplace?

Many people view seminaries as largely irrelevant to the realities of survival in a harsh and unforgiving society. What are we accomplishing in graduate theological education that contributes to the betterment of society? What compelling answer/achievement can the faculty, administration, and trustees offer to friends and foes alike? A strong case for theological education can be made, I believe, through a coherent curriculum that communicates not only what is basic to Christianity, but also a message that can humanize our lives and help us to be more authentic with one another. But as Farley and others have indicated, our curriculum is fragmented and we are sending out graduates without a clear message that commands an audience. We have replaced a message of redemption with a therapy of accommodation to our circumstances in life.

## Teaching What Is Basic to Christianity

Our task is to get back to basics in theological education through the biblical message of reconciliation. We must find our rightful voice in a needy society where brokenness and despair exist. Tomorrow's seminary curriculum must center itself unapologetically on exegeting and communicating what is basic to Christianity. The seminary curriculum ought to express its theological coherence within the encompassing theme of *forgiveness*. The power of forgiveness is a missing ingredient in humanizing a world torn by individual and collective self-interest with the capacity for self-destruction. The end goal of a theological curriculum is to graduate seminarians who have a realistic grasp on what forgiveness can accomplish in an unforgiving society, where "God talk" and Main Street realities can confront each other. Herein lies our unique message and mission as a graduate theological school within a society plagued by violence, greed, and endless searching for its soul.

Do Christians have a monopoly on forgiveness? No, and we will need allies throughout our global village. I believe forgiveness ought to be emphasized in future interfaith dialogue within our multicultural society.[8] Practicing forgiveness enhances the quality of life and humanizes our existence with dignity. It points to the essential reality of our lives, namely, *relationships*—with others and with God. Unfortunately, the sad fact is that these relationships are often strained, tarnished, and dysfunctional. If our students learn to understand the dynamics and dimensions of forgiveness in human life, they will indeed have a message that is relevant; when applied skillfully and meaningfully within society this message can make a positive difference for good. Simply put, Christian theological education that is scripturally informed teaches that we can't be good without God's grace of forgiving love manifested in Christ (John 2:7–17).

Christian theological educators may agree or disagree on the breadth or narrowness of this interpretation of biblical faith as forgiveness, but I hope all of us will concede that Christianity cannot be explained without forgiveness. Through our trinitarian understanding of the Christian faith, we believe that Jesus Christ is forgiveness in the flesh. Furthermore, we believe that forgiving one another is the human way of loving one another. This is not an easy path, but following its incarnate Messenger can liberate, fulfill, and bring us joy.

Some might feel that forgiveness is neither realistic nor applicable in this unfair and unjust world; why should theological schools stake their existence upon a curriculum of forgiveness? No doubt at times forgiveness can seem too anemic an approach before the harsh realities and power politics of organizations and nations. Even so, can you imagine what the quality of life would be like without forgiveness? The answer is hell. Living on a global island that is vengeful and suspicious is a hellish existence when forgiveness is alien to human life. The realities of forgiveness and its healing power are unique lessons that seminaries can teach and communicate in today's world of distrust and vengeance. As Archbishop Desmond Tutu has rightly said, "Forgiveness is taking seriously the awfulness of what has happened when you are treated unfairly, it is opening the door for the other person to have a chance to begin again. Without forgiveness, resentment builds in us, and resentment . . . turns into hostility and anger. Hatred eats away at our well-being."[9] Furthermore, Tutu points out that our own well-being must be tied to the well-being of others if harmony is to be established. "Anything that subverts this harmony is injurious, not just to the community, but to all of us, and therefore forgiveness is an absolute necessity for continual human existence."[10]

We can discuss peacemaking within our society forever, but without the practice of forgiveness, vengeance will continue to outweigh the urgency for reconciliation. Here in the United States we have numerous displaced workers who are victims of global competition, downsizing and technological change. We have an aging population threatened by rising costs; there is also the unceasing battle for basic rights of women, minorities, and the physically disadvantaged. Why then does forgiveness sound weak and ineffective to remedy these realities? Or is there in the message of forgiveness a better way to develop social, economic, and political policies that will promote a more promising future?

Of course, skeptics wonder if theological education organized under any theme will be able to cope sufficiently with the real world. It seems that theological communities have found their own language and practice inadequate as they adopt current terms and causes such as liberation, feminization, democratic socialism, democratic capitalism, individualism, compassionate conservatism, deconstruction, communitarianism, and self-actualization. In the marketplace of ideas, theological insight is often hidden under a bushel of ideologies; the social pronouncements of ecclesiastical organizations sometimes simply echo modified versions of the Democratic or Republican Party platforms.

The uniqueness of the church's witness is often lost among the prevailing moods of society, and the theological school is often pressured to add courses that respond to various perceived deficiencies in society. We are in danger of losing control of our curriculum when we trade off or neglect basic convictions in order to provide Band-Aids for the wounds of society in our efforts to save ourselves from irrelevance. Ironically, our attempt to address contemporary problems by adding courses to the curriculum still leaves us with insufficient core courses central to our message. At the same time, so few students are usually able to sign up for the elective courses that some faculty feel the solution is another curriculum revision. The practice of adding or subtracting courses fosters a dispersed curriculum, pushing many faculty members into their specific interests and seemingly contributing to our alienation from one another. A sense of cohesive structure implies much more than a congenial atmosphere of uncritical tolerance.

## Is Forgiveness a Sufficient Curriculum for a Fragmented World?

You may be questioning whether a theological curriculum ought to have a single focus. Haven't we in recent times emphasized globalization, peacemaking, liberation, and environmental concerns? How long would the theme of forgiveness last? Can it adequately capture the reforming history behind our common ecumenical heritage that calls us into discipleship and service?

I believe forgiveness is the necessary prerequisite for any sustained effort at peacemaking, globalization, liberation, etc. There is no *shalom* without forgiveness in a fragmented world. To live by the forgiveness of God without forgiving one's enemy is inconceivable. This is true for persons, organizations, and nations.[11] Forgiveness is not only a substantive matter in Christian theology, it can be the most durable thread from which theological education achieves unity and strength. God's forgiveness and human forgiveness are intimately interwoven (Matthew 5 and 18). Baptism, Eucharist, and penance are mediating channels by which divine forgiveness is expressed. The climactic prayer of Jesus on the cross for the forgiveness of his enemies (Luke 23:34) highlights divine power and human need at the same time. Forgiveness comes from God and has the power to reconcile not only persons, but also classes, nations, and races. We have only experienced a glimpse of the potential power and reconciliation that comes through forgiveness.

Only genuine forgiveness that is painful at times will enable us to be touched with the healing realities of our gospel hymns as we encounter the real world of daily events. Forgiveness accepts the reality of sin, a reality often denied in our sophisticated but disillusioned society. We try to lessen the sting of sin and thereby dilute our need for forgiveness. We search for an endless list of panaceas to rationalize our shortcomings, while society continues to be suspicious, vengeful, and unforgiving. Today's latest fad—spirituality—promises a serenity that often bypasses the need for forgiveness. People often wish to avoid the painful struggle that is involved in genuine forgiveness; the price of humility involved in the process is too costly. How to convey this need for forgiveness is an educational challenge facing every theological school community. Seminaries and divinity schools can begin by developing a curriculum that intentionally graduates students who have a grasp of the dynamics and dimensions of forgiveness and can encourage its practice within society. A proper curriculum of forgiveness will draw together theology and experience, encouraging us to integrate both if we wish to fortify Christian practices in a fragmented society.

The seminary is more than a sanctuary for scholarship; it is also a laboratory for the practice of forgiveness. There are many dimensions to forgiveness that need to be studied and digested. During the student's first year of study, a conscious effort should be made to exegete the theme of forgiveness in biblical courses as well as introductory studies in other disciplines. In the second year, a field-based course could be proposed to integrate the history, theology, ethics, and spirituality of forgiveness with explicit emphasis on how local churches can become centers of forgiveness. In actual parish life, problems of forgiveness cannot be outlined in a course syllabus, but come in complex and unexpected packages.

In the senior year, small group seminars under faculty leadership could focus on studying the enemies of forgiveness such as prejudice, greed, power, relativism, third world debt, pride, favoritism, etc., through case studies. These examples will illustrate realistically how forgiveness can be applied to power and turf issues, and problems of greed and prejudice which have torn apart families, businesses, and nations. There are also the questions of blind pride and national intolerance that need to be addressed through understanding and the practice of forgiveness.

### DISCUSSION STARTER

Curriculum discussion within theological school communities can be endless; at times relationships are strained and much time is spent with little to show for it afterwards. Each school must be willing to pay a price to enter into this long discussion process. The rules for dialogue will need to be learned if our conversations are to be more than a series of debates. We cannot speak of a school's mission without reference to the curriculum, asking if it provides Christian leaders with a message that has universal application among churches and communities. This does not mean a "one size fits all" approach in the application of forgiveness, but it does imply that there is a national as well as global need for forgiveness that will transform individuals and nations to be more humane. Our intent is to make human life more human as exemplified and demonstrated by Jesus. A forgiving theology will empower us to transcend our self-imposed prisons and ghettos of isolation and suspicion individually and collectively.

Does your theological curriculum have a focus? If not, would you like it to have a focus? Have you identified your own biases for a curriculum and the outcomes you desire from a theological education? What content does a theological curriculum need to have to encourage believers in their journey of faith?

# Chapter 6

# Making the World Your Classroom

*T*heological schools for the most part see their task as educating leaders to serve local churches. The new challenge, known as a "missional" emphasis, calls us to acquire an attitude of passion for the world as God has shown it in Christ. Therefore, churches and theological schools must more seriously consider the needs of the entire world as well as the local church. Are seminaries ready to accept the world as their classroom and to take into account the demands and budget considerations of such an outlook?

Australian Robert Banks is among a growing number of theological educators urging us to rethink theological education from a mission perspective.[1] Banks converts the noun "mission" into "missional" to highlight the "missional approach" in understanding both the content and delivery of theological education in the future. The "missional" model of theological education is "an education undertaken with a view to what God is doing in the world, considered from a global perspective."[2] It "places the main emphasis on theological *mission*, on hands-on partnership in ministry based on interpreting the tradition and reflecting on practice with a strong spiritual and communal dimension."[3]

This "missional outlook" tends to be wholly or partly field-based in a global as well as a local setting, and places its emphasis outside the classroom. Banks and others who share this view want the learning community of theological schools extended beyond the campus gates so that students, faculty, and administrators might experience their ministry in the context of God's classroom—the world. Access to this world-oriented classroom would occur not after one's degree is earned, but during the process of one's education. The spirit behind this missional approach to theological education is found in the text of John 3:16: "For God so loved the world that he gave his only Son, so that everyone who believes in him may not perish but may have eternal life." The context for theological education is not restricted to the classroom, but encourages us to be in the world at the same time.

## The Church as Mission

The church and theological schools stand today—as they always have—in a changing world. In the midst of this world, the believer's constant mission is to interpret the event of Jesus Christ and to intercede in his name in a world that is materially and spiritually in need. Living in the context of change, the world never ceases being a mission field. No longer should we understand mission to mean being sent to distant lands; it also means being sent to our neighborhoods and the urban streets of our cities.

As graduate schools of the church, seminaries are to provide educated leadership to enable the church to address this wider and continual mission. The school's specific task is to educate astute doers and interpreters of the Word of God for a clamoring world. As Christ was sent, so too are we commissioned to go forth under the sign of his cross into the marketplaces of contemporary society, equipped to tell the story encapsulated in John 3:16.

Yet, quite honestly, we often feel powerless when confronted by the world. The raw realities are intimidating—even crushing at times—eclipsing the tiny oasis of hope wherever two, three, or more are gathered in Christ's name. Every day we are caught struggling with our love/hate emotions toward the world. Sometimes we are at a loss to know just how to respond as we fight for survival. Others of us are so preoccupied with skirmishes within our homes, churches, or seminary communities that we do not have the energy to confront the larger issues of society. The church's current tendency toward spiritual inwardness may be a sign of our poor health. We are losing sight of the larger world that God loves.

During a trip to Egypt, I walked with Emile Zaki, an Egyptian pastor and teacher, from his church in a worker's district of Cairo to the nearby train station. Though it took only twenty-five minutes, that walk took me along one of the most exotic pathways of my life, a new world of sights, sounds, and smells. Preoccupied with my own and others' physical safety, I became momentarily "lost" in the multitude of humanity pressing in upon me, shouting and struggling for their slice of bread. How in God's name, I thought, can anyone proclaim John 3:16 to this unruly mob and expect a hearing? The scene violated my sense of balance and upset my psychic equilibrium. I suspect first-time visitors walking our city streets in New York, Los Angeles, and Chicago might have similar feelings of insecurity and fear.

This encounter in Cairo reminds me that most of twentieth-century theology originated on the cleanly swept streets of Basel, Zurich, Edinburgh, Tübingen, and Marburg—a long way, both psychically and psychologically, from the crowded cities and alleys of Seoul, Hong Kong, Cairo, or Bombay.

The question, then, is whether these theologies of the Occident really apply to the non-Western societies where the vast majority of the world's population resides. Is our present understanding of God's love too culturally bound, emotionally as well as intellectually?

The biblical reality is that God loves the world and all its humanity. The more difficult question is whether we do. Are we protecting ourselves from the real world, hiding within the sanctuaries of our middle-class homes and suburban shopping centers?

We know that affluent Christians are a minority when compared to the world's poor Christians and non-Christians. We are not so willing to admit that we are simply too frightened to venture out among the majority. Even faithful missionaries, like us, live at times by double standards, giving voice to the oppressed and poor, but requiring middle-class standards of shelter in order to maintain a sense of security. I do not intend with this to be judgmental, but only to point out our dilemma: On the one hand, we are challenged to love and accept the world as God does; yet on the other hand, we are aware that oppressive conditions and dirty surroundings weaken our resolve and undermine our witness.

There is, I'm afraid, far more complacency, fear, and fatigue in our church and seminary communities today than we are willing to admit! We seem to want rewards and recognition whenever we do something "extra" for Jesus. Perhaps Jürgen Moltmann is correct in suggesting that today's Christianity demands nothing. The product of organized Christianity today is an institutionalized absence of commitment. A Christianity without demands points to a church without vitality; it suggests an irrelevant gospel that is largely ignored in the marketplaces of the world.

What can we do to raise our level of commitment to the rest of the world? This is the paramount question facing theological education. Are we willing to become church leaders who will make a difference? Are we willing to be more demanding of ourselves, working as diligently as our rhetoric claims? Are we willing to learn our theology in the midst of God's classroom—the world? This is what a missional approach to theological education invites us to do. Are we willing to understand our churches and theological schools as "missional" in nature?

## Acquiring the Spirit of John 3:16
## within Our Seminaries and Churches

We ourselves must seek to become leaders who will make a difference; we cannot stand around waiting for our neighbors to take the initiative. The issue is whether the church wants to encourage challenging and creative leadership to confront the status quo and take risks for the world that God loves? Accepting the world around us beginning with our urban neighborhoods is the first major hurdle for most of us. In Seoul, a Korean pastor asked me, "How can you tell us how to revitalize our churches when the churches in your own country are declining? Should we learn from you, or should you learn from us?" It was certainly a fair question. Christianity is expanding in his country and in Africa, but waning in Europe and in North America.

My response begins with my earlier call for theological recovery of the power of forgiveness to humanize our global society. Unforgiving and suspicious people measure power and influence only in financial and political terms. Christians must rediscover a deeper gratitude for God's love that was displayed so completely on the cross. Only when we become true practitioners of such forgiveness and understand our indebtedness to God, whom we can never repay, will we recognize that God's grace demands our highest priority and sacrificial loyalty. Most of us simply do not have that personal level of commitment, and the curricula in our theological schools do not reflect the importance of forgiveness. We come before the Divine Presence with other agenda, and only passively participate in our liturgical confessions of sin and pardon. Why, then, do we wonder where the passion for our faith has gone?

Once our emotional and confessional priorities are recognized, we can investigate the specific situations before us. No prescription is worth much without adequate diagnosis—which requires a comprehensive investigation. Contemporary society has few "small and simple" problems; our concerns are interrelated with deeply buried and tangled root causes. A helpful theological diagnosis requires sufficient pooling of intellect and expertise from members of the congregation, community, and beyond. Clergy and faculty must not be shy in asking for help from the widest possible circle of people to understand and help correct difficult situations.

We must also be willing to commit and sacrifice ourselves, whatever price is demanded. Most of us, unfortunately, hold ourselves back with conditional commitments to mask unspoken doubts. Our willingness to risk ourselves without reservation will liberate us to be disciples—unencumbered by the excess baggage of a tourist, we will instead be satisfied with the napsack of a pilgrim.

Finally, we need to develop in our schools and parishes small groups of persons who share a common direction and vision. These groups, with the aid of faculty and pastoral leadership, can set an example of commitment to the community. Acting in the spirit of Jesus' early disciples, they will work to give authentic witness through their actions of love, forgiveness, and care for all of

God's people. To begin this "missional" vision in our schools and parishes, we need to nurture an ethos for mission that prepares individuals during their school years. The curriculum plays a key role here, but also opportunities must be presented to continue the student's learning experience beyond the classroom.[4]

If we follow a process as outlined above, we will elevate the level of commitment within our schools and churches in our outreach to the world. But will our communities tolerate the enthusiastic and visionary leadership that can be nurtured by these small groups? Some would prefer more passive participants in our communities of learning and worship. This leaves us with two unanswered questions: Do our schools and churches desire passionate leaders for our communities of faith? And are theological educators willing and able to equip seminarians with a "missional" vision to love God's world in the spirit of Christ?

### Educating Students in a Wider World

Developing leadership that is in touch with the world requires modifying the traditional format of theological education. While we must maintain our commitment to the basic disciplines of the seminary curriculum, we can provide opportunities to students that earlier generations of church leadership missed. For instance, some theological schools offer joint degree programs in which dual competency can be gained in cooperation with professional graduate schools of other universities. These academic programs enable students to complement their theological and biblical studies with courses in public management and policy, law, music, social work, information and library science, or health-care administration. Graduates with a wider variety of academic coursework can relate more knowledgeably to varied contemporary issues in society.

At Pittsburgh, we are educating our students to look outward by inviting to our campus international guests who have varied perspectives in mission and evangelism. Our curriculum also includes courses on the interrelationship between economics and belief systems, peacemaking and justice issues, the ethics of technology, and how to relate biblical values to the business-oriented culture that surrounds us. Opportunities also exist for faculty members and students to meet with attorneys, doctors, and business executives for collaboration and consultation on areas of mutual concern through a Center on Business, Religion, and Public Life, which stimulates dialogue with decision-makers in the public and private sectors of society. A World Mission Initiative program promotes mission concerns and exchanges abroad. A Metro-Urban Institute provides field-based classroom experiences to assist in understanding urban dynamics for ministry for those who live and work in our cities. These are all efforts to engage seminarians in the contemporary issues of society, helping to bring the world into our classroom experience.

Seminaries are blessed today with a large number of "second career" students from business, education, law, engineering, and architecture. Enrollment of second and third career students is approximately half of the student body at most seminaries. Both in and out of the classroom, these seasoned students are in conversation with faculty and younger students, widening everyone's horizons to the realities of the marketplace.

Strategic plans at our institution call for establishing effective networks with theological leadership abroad, along with contacts with labor, government, and corporate leadership at home. This global and local networking provides seminarians with learning opportunities through summer internships to enlarge the student's world and to motivate our students to find creative and collegial patterns of partnership within our expanding global village. Our intent is to have students more alert to outside issues and their impact upon congregations in our shrinking world. Hopefully, this wider outlook will prepare tomorrow's leadership to have a better understanding of our global context and to be more willing to share God's love with a waiting world. We need to be more mission-minded in our approach to theological education if we wish to enrich our churches and prepare them to welcome immigrants who will be their future neighbors.

Amidst an ever-changing world, we must continually remind ourselves that the commitment of the church and seminary is to an on-going reformation—*ecclesia reformata et semper reformanda*. The church "reformed and always reforming" is the hallmark of a pilgrim's theology, an outlook that ought to be encouraged in all our theological schools. Without a reforming bias in theological education, we would be unable to fulfill the challenge of John 3:16 in realistic ways. Those of us in the seminaries need to wrestle vigorously with the text of John 3:16 through coursework, in our dialogues on and off campus, and through chatrooms around the world. At the same time, we must become more astute students of society—beginning with our own neighborhoods—as we grasp the social and economic dimensions of community life and address the competing belief systems within our societies.

The need and call for theologically educated leaders is greater than ever; their task is not only to interpret, but also to be engaged in the world from the standpoint of God's agenda. Through the church's extensive network we are called to carry out the spirit of John 3:16. And we can do so in the confidence that Christ has gone before us and the Spirit of God is behind us, upholding us daily. The question confronting you and me is whether we are willing to love and accept the world as God did in Jesus Christ. To answer affirmatively places us under the biblical sanction to graduate leaders who have the passion and compassion to share God's forgiving love with humankind everywhere.

## DISCUSSION STARTER

*I*s Banks creating an unnecessary neologism with the term "missional" for "mission," causing academic hairsplitting to highlight a "missional" model of theological education in contrast to the *classical model* of Farley et al., or the *vocation model* of Joseph Hough, John Cobb, and Max Stackhouse, or the *dialectical model* of Charles Wood, David Kelsey, and Rebecca Chopp, or the *confessional model* of George Shriner and Richard A. Muller?[5]

The *classical* model in theological education places emphasis on moral and cognitive wisdom; the *vocational* model relates the Christian story to contemporary issues with an emphasis on discernment; the *dialectical* model relates theological studies to the ethos or context where theology takes place, seeking insight along with cognition; the *confessional* model places emphasis on gaining theological information and understanding, seeking revelatory knowledge to express in doctrinal and ethical form; and the *missional* model seeks to acquire "cognitive, spiritual, and practical obedience" in the classroom and in the world. The emphasis in this model is on service. Without question, there is something to learn from each model; I suspect that no composite "super-model" of theological education exists that will satisfy all interested parties.

It is more to the point, then, to indicate that the challenge of John 3:16 places a burden on all models of theological education (including the "missional") to uncover the exegetical depth of this text, requiring students and faculty to discern the width, height, breadth, and depth of God's love which is beyond our comprehension. No single group of believers or theological methodologies can understand fully the amazing aspects of God's redeeming grace. Only as we become saturated in the mystery and wisdom of God's love in Christ can we hope to become faithful followers and leaders interpreting and demonstrating the outreach of God's forgiving love. How fortunate we are to believe that in life and in death we belong to God! This is the bottom line of all theological reflection. From the perspective of John 3:16, we must never lose sight in all our studies that the world is both God's mission field and God's classroom. How can we teach and demonstrate to our students and ourselves a love for the world without being captured and transformed by it? Has your theological school enabled you to cultivate a mission outlook for your ministry? If not, why not?

# Chapter 7

# The Globalization and Multiculturalization of Theological Education

### Tomorrow's Parishioners: Abigael and Rachel

Abigael is a lovable six-month-old baby, the daughter of Cristina and Miguel who live in Nogales, Mexico. I met them through my participation in a Summer Institute on Globalization in Theological Education sponsored by the ATS. I watched baby Abigael crawl on the dirt floor under her mother's watchful eye, and minutes later I observed mother Cristina pick up Abigael and nurse her while serving customers at a small candy stand that was part of their improvised living quarters.

Miguel is a leader of his *colonia*, a squatters' community occupying invaded vacant land belonging to absentee landowners. "We are a proud people," Miguel said. "We want to pay for the land we have seized, but the absentee landowners and government officials won't respond to our requests. This inaction by the powerful makes us more frustrated, forcing us to invade the land and possess it. We wish it were otherwise." Near the *colonia* are the *maquiladora* industries. These are foreign companies (over 2,200 in number) located along the border between the United States and Mexico, providing over half a million jobs for Mexican citizens. Approximately 70 percent of the foreign companies located in Nogales are American owned. The Mexican government's design in establishing the *maquiladora* industries was to assist their country's weak economy and unemployment. The arrival of thousands of workers from across Mexico for these jobs has contributed to an acute housing shortage along the border.

We visited Sumex, owned by Xerox and one of the many industries located in Nogales, and talked with the American general manager who also gave us a tour of the plant where nearly 200 Mexicans are employed to assemble typewriter ribbon. The manager's twofold objective: to operate a cost effective plant, and at the same time to provide a humane working environment. He is concerned with the 14 percent turnover in his work force, which is actually lower than other local industries. The average age of the workers is eighteen; the minimum beginning wage is approximately $4.00 per day; average earnings among experienced *maquiladora* workers is $5.70 a day. The manager wishes he could pay more, but the company tries to stay competitive against even lower wages in the Philippines, islands of the Pacific, and China. "Xerox," he said, "has to keep pace with the realities of today's global economy." By maintaining plants like this in Mexico, U.S. companies are able to keep prices down and hold on to their worldwide customers; in an economically oriented world, loyalty counts for little and national boundaries for even less.

The manager went on to say, "Low-cost general labor in Nogales allows America to stay competitive worldwide, passing on the savings to consumers at home. The *maquiladora* industries serve as a buffer, providing needed jobs for Mexicans and preventing the erosion of higher paying skilled jobs in the United States."

Is this presentation an acceptable explanation? After all, 60 percent of the *maquiladora* workers live in the *colonia* and have inadequate housing. Their homes, improvised from discarded trash, are in stark contrast to the well-designed plant owned by Xerox. Abigael's globalized future on the U.S./Mexican border does not look very promising to me.

Nearly two thousand miles from Abigael lives three-month-old Rachel in a Chicago suburb. She was born to Lois and Dennis, my daughter and son-in-law; she is our first grandchild and, of course, we think she is beautiful. Rachel is being raised in a middle-class neighborhood, a different lifestyle from Abigael's in Nogales. Both are children of today's global economy; both have loving parents who are deeply concerned for their child's welfare. Both are living in urban settings where wealth and poverty are in close proximity. In today's globalized context, Rachel and Abigael are neighbors, though they may never personally meet each other. Nevertheless, their contrasting standards will impact each other in this complex, interdependent, globalized society.

The globalization of today's economy also affects Abigael's and Rachel's parents. Cheap labor in Mexico means Americans and others can buy consumer goods at lower costs. In Nogales, Cristina and Miguel are grateful that their neighbors have work in the *maquiladora* industries and therefore have pesos to buy candy. Neither Miguel, Cristina, nor their neighbors are lazy people; they are asking only for the opportunity to make their lives more humane, not necessarily to emulate American standards and lifestyle.

Who then is the enemy? Is it Americans who are the recipients of the goods and services made possible through this global economy? Perhaps it is too simplistic to point to business and consumers as the enemy. To what extent is Miguel, the community leader, the enemy as well? While I'm deeply empathetic to his goals to improve the quality of life in his squatters' community, to what extent has he contributed negatively to the situation by refusing to compromise realistically with the landowners and government? Our visit was too brief to assess the situation. To what extent is the establishment the real enemy—the landowners and government officials accused of taking bribes? We could go on and on as we untangle the complicated maze created by a global society where there are no simple solutions, but a crying need on all sides to struggle for justice. Defining the complexities is more difficult than it appears at times.

## We Are No Longer Islands unto Ourselves

Abigael and Rachel's future in a globalized world is unfolding in our midst, not only on the U.S./Mexican border, but also in the present struggle for peace and justice in the Middle East, in Central and South America, Asia, Eastern Europe, and the countries of Africa. Realizing this, in June 1990 ATS passed a new standard for globalization that is currently part of the accrediting process for theological institutions.[1] Its intention is to expose seminarians and faculty to a more comprehensive context of global realities in which to do theology and to practice ministry.

Within such globalization, theological educators are still in search of an encompassing definition of their task. It seems that globalization doesn't have the same meaning for everyone. For some, globalization involves a fourfold task: *evangelism*, *ecumenism*, *interfaith dialogue*, and *pursuing justice* on behalf of the poor and oppressed. These elements interact and intersect with each other, calling for greater flexibility in our encounters with one another. For others, globalization implies that we no longer tolerate ignorance and provincialism; it directs us to questions regarding the church's mission to the entire inhabited world. For this group, globalization flows directly from the universality of the gospel and the consequent plurality of human responses; it is the search for universals in values, beliefs, and practices. Globalization calls us to be transnational and transcultural and underlies the interconnectedness of our world and nature. This implies rethinking our division of the world as first, second, third, fourth, etc. Each of these worlds not only intersects the others, but also exists within others. In short, globalization is entering into and testifying to the catholic scope of God's saving rule in Jesus Christ. For all parties, globalization is striving for wholeness, overcoming fragmentary approaches to the environment as well as economic and political issues, while upholding the ethno-cultural distinctions among ourselves.

Globalization is opposed to monoculturalism in any form. It is the honest attempt to look into the eyes of strangers and discover their personhood, to regard others as humans, not objects across ethnic, racial, gender, and class lines. It is the attempt to look beyond our own selfish understanding of reality and to be other directed. It means letting go, seeking to be less in control, and dropping our paternalism. Globalization encourages us to increase our ability and skill to learn from other realities and perspectives; to discard our own particular pair of glasses and to see through the various lenses of our global neighbors. Globalization is widening our horizons through cross-cultural experiences, a process of multiculturalization.

Of course, none of these above definitions of globalization is complete by itself. However, the process of defining globalization is important; it enables us to give attention to theological and pedagogical implications for seminary education. For instance, to think theologically on globalization calls us to confess:

1. *God is global.* We must transcend the ethnic, cultural, political, and economic entrapment of God (Acts 10:30–43). The mysterious being of God is beyond our comprehension.
2. *The gospel is global.* The biblical message (John 3:16) offers the gift of redemption for everyone without exception.
3. *Greed is global.* God's generosity, which is our good news in Christ, confronts greed in its diverse manifestations.
4. *Scripture is global.* The Bible is the vehicle through which a diverse body of people (Galatians 3:27–29) can discuss their search for meaning together.
5. *The Church is a global network.* The grassroots network of churches worldwide might well be the envy of many business and government agencies. The basic local church can remind clergy to be responsive to all people, working through people on behalf of people who are created in God's image.
6. *Christians are a global minority.* Christianity is a minority faith among the sum total of the world's religious believers. It has been observed with some justification that those who understand only their own religion understand none. In addition to critically examining many Christian theologies—liberation, black, feminist, evangelical, liberal, confessional, etc.—we must seriously encounter and dialogue with Jews, Hindus, Muslims, Buddhists, and those of other faiths. Today, there are at least as many Muslims in the United States as there are Episcopalians and Presbyterians, and it is estimated that Islam will soon replace Judaism as the second largest religion in North America. Religious pluralism will continue to grow. Buddhism, Islam, and Hinduism, once considered foreign religions, will increasingly be a part of the religious landscape in North America.

## When Faculty Become Students Again

All of these intra- and inter-faith realities carry pedagogical implications for theological educators. First, we must realize that homogeneity within seminary communities breeds intellectual myopia and tends to perpetuate a narrow perspective that reflects the dominant culture and worldview on campus. In most of our cases, this means that our American adaptation of Europeanized theological insights, categories, and criteria will need fresh scrutiny and reevaluation.

Second, we tend to be too "lecture-bound" in our methodology, asking students to conceptualize their thoughts through reports, journals, essay exams, and term papers. We must search for other means of learning. Faculty must uncover more student-centered approaches to learning. This need becomes even more acute given the wide age span of seminarians today and their diverse range of experiences and skills, not to mention also the growing impact of the Internet on global and local theological education. Technology has saturated us with information, but learning is more than information gathering; it also involves transforming experiences that usher in fresh outlooks, removing previous priorities and prejudices from us. Faculty need to become students to discover how students learn today.

The faculty must lead the way and illustrate to students that they are capable of learning and changing and are not tied to predictable responses repeated each year. Professors must listen as well as lecture. Perhaps faculty should distribute their lectures earlier for study and free up class sessions for discussion; in this way, faculty and students can interactively bring renewed vigor and excitement to theological education. Or if everyone has access to a computer, encourage students to download lectures and ask them to send their questions by email prior to class discussion and then organize their inquiries into a "response lecture" during class time. This could be a more dynamic format for students and faculty. It could also lead to insightful possibilities and unexpected discoveries for everyone.

Third, we need to provide greater opportunities for our students to learn experientially. Excursions and immersion in alien cultures, whether abroad or in urban and rural settings at home, need to be designed and executed. If this implies that an institution needs to reconsider scheduling of courses as well as curriculum offerings, such discussions should commence without delay within the school's structures. One of the goals of the World Mission Initiative (WMI) program at our seminary is to encourage and arrange cross-cultural experiences with faculty involvement and internships to expose students to the globalization of the church's ministry and widen their range of possible ministries in the future.

Global and multicultural awareness in theological education challenges us to move closer to the grassroots struggle that leads to new alliances and friendships at home and abroad. We cannot afford to theologize from a distance as the educated elite. Everything and everyone is interconnected in a globalized society; isolated responses and solo styles of leadership are not sufficient.[2]

Fourth, we must sensitize ourselves through diverse materials—case studies, computer networking, video films, tapes, drama, readings, and the utilization of our students' past experiences—to create exciting teachable moments. How many opportunities do we miss through the passive forms of instruction practiced in many theological institutions today? Even our times of fellowship and socializing can be times to further inform one another of our personal journeys of faith, thereby enriching our classroom understanding as well.

Fifth, a more global and multicultural approach to teaching theology and the practice of ministry will call for more interdisciplinary and multidisciplinary teaching teams that will enhance the learning experience for faculty as well as for students. This will encourage greater openness in pedagogy that will be far more supportive in building a multicultural classroom experience for everyone, linking the local and global aspects of what is being taught. Such an approach to teaching in our theological schools would balance the "Lone Ranger" mentality where the professor's expertise places the student in a passive role as a recipient of information, thereby neglecting the personal and cultural dimensions the student brings to the hermeneutical task in the classroom. Faculty who are sensitive to these factors and have sufficient self-confidence will be open to having their assumptions challenged as they engage students through the complex maze of cultural and global backgrounds that may be present in the classroom. Faculty who are also open to learning will create a more stimulating environment for everyone, as professors and students become learners from their respective backgrounds. Such an attitude to learning can be truly exciting and transformational for all.[3]

In short, the globalization and multiculturalization of baby Abigael and baby Rachel is inevitable. Today's children will be more globalized, computerized, and multiculturalized than all preceding generations. Can theological education meet the challenge and provide Abigael and Rachel with pastoral leadership that indeed understands the changing and interconnective context of witnessing to the gospel on both local and global levels at the same time? For the sake of future generations, we have a moral responsibility to be students, professors, and pastors who are becoming globalized and multiculturalized as the amazing grace of God unfolds before us.

## DISCUSSION STARTER

What is your understanding of the educational process in an interconnected world? How can we expect theological students to connect their studies with the world when we hold so firmly to our disciplinary boundaries? Will successful teaching in our schools include a more holistic hermeneutic? Will a more multidisciplinary approach enhance the creativity within the classroom and challenge the imagination of all, transforming oftentimes a hierarchical classroom into a learning community where instructor and students strive together to relate the gospel to situations that are increasingly global and multicultural wherever we live?

Professor Dale T. Irvin of New York Theological Seminary sums up this open-ended pedagogy by reminding us that traditionally, "the texts that provided the major substance for the course were the professor's lecture and the assigned readings. In the multidisciplinary, multicultural classroom, however, the text becomes the discussion itself that takes place within the class, as new configurations of knowledge and new relationships emerge. Lecture and assigned readings come to serve more as pretexts for learning. Here again the interaction among pretext, text, and context is a mode of intertextuality that will advance dialogue among disciplines and practices, doing so across the boundaries of culture, race, gender, class, and sexual orientation."[4] I suspect that many theological educators are already engaged in an open-ended pedagogy as understood by Irvin. The question is how large a role this teaching methodology should have within the culture of our respective theological schools. How traditional or experimental do we need to be in our pedagogies as we pursue truth, define reality, and seek to be relevant within our global societies?

Chapter 8

# Expanding the Horizons
# of Seminary Education

## Continuing Education for the People of God

*W*hen I entered seminary in 1955, theological education was taught primarily from a clerical paradigm. That is to say, the seminary was viewed as an academic and professional school to educate future clergy and church educators. The administration and faculty saw themselves as preparing leaders for ministry and mission at home and abroad. Continuing education programs for laity and clergy were often considered in those days an added burden and normally beyond the proper scope of the school; it was felt that continuing education ought to be left to denominational officials and religious education programs in the churches.

At the same time, seminaries and divinity schools also saw themselves as graduate schools of the academy dedicated to teaching, research, and publications, and their ecclesiastical obligations tended to be subordinate to the goals of higher education. Publications by the faculty for a general church audience were not encouraged; academic publications were given a higher profile. Today these same theological graduate schools, in the face of churches' reductions in educational programming and financial support, and no longer assured of receiving scarce denominational dollars, have pragmatically, if not theologically and professionally, convinced themselves that they need to serve a wider public. There is a growing suspicion that it might also be the right thing to reach beyond seminarians and graduate research students to serve all God's people, assuming greater responsibility for educating a wider and more representative audience. This can be said to be a prelude for what is now referred to as "public theology," by which we mean providing theological and ethical insight and challenges to a far-ranging audience in the public arena.

Some theological educators are now asking whether we are sponsoring too many continuing education programs and moving too far from the primary mission of theological schools. Behind their question is the old feeling that seminary education ought to mean clergy education. The answer depends of course on how closely we wish to be identified with a clerical paradigm. Frankly, I am glad to see more parishioners and members of the general public attending seminary events and classes. I believe a metamorphosis is slowly taking place among traditional theological schools; we now see the need to open our doors to the larger public that is more representative of the church's membership and to invite intelligent inquirers who are searching for an abiding and relevant faith for themselves. For some who have come, our continuing education programs and courses have performed the function of a catechumenate, leading later to their membership or renewed commitment to the church.

Take, for example, Regent College in Vancouver, British Columbia, which with its Anglican roots was actually designed to be an "unseminary" for the laity. It officially sees itself as "An International Graduate School of Christian Studies." While its lay emphasis continues to be strong, it has in recent years also taken on the clerical paradigm of traditional schools in preparing persons for ordained ministry. However, what impresses me about Regent College is its large and exciting summer school offerings, largely for the laity, which average over five hundred attendees. Many lay persons use their vacation time to study the faith seriously. The Vancouver School of Theology, a neighbor of Regent College, also offers a stimulating summer program that has clergy and laity studying together; in fact, the two theological institutions in Vancouver co-sponsor some courses in spite of their contrasting theological positions. This unique ecumenical cooperation illustrates the vision found in these two schools to address common needs for nurturing among the people of God, where clergy and laity can rediscover their partnership.

Bringing theological education to all the people of God—laity as well as clergy—ought to become the normative practice among our theological schools. I believe the shift to such a "people of God" paradigm would be strongly supported by churches. We need to overcome the unhealthy perception that "the church is owned by the clergy."[1] The Reformers wanted to return the church to the people of God, to unchain the scriptures from the pulpit and to translate it into the vernacular for the sake of all God's people. Professional theological education, in spite of all its positive contributions, gives the public impression of dividing the people of God into a church of clergy and a church of laity. It implies that clergy primarily, not laity, are privileged to understand the secrets of God's revelation, trained as they are in the language of ecclesiastical tradition.

We depend on the laity to support theological schools financially, even while we restrict their active participation within our programs. The popular view of a "seminary" tends to create distance from the laity who might like to participate in advanced theological education without feeling the obligation to enter the ranks of professional clergy. When a lay person enrolls in a seminary, we draw the quick conclusion that he or she is becoming a pastor. Seminaries and divinity schools should also be seen as centers of graduate theological study welcoming all God's people. Making this shift alone in our perception would be a renewing spirit for churches and theological schools.

Out of necessity, Catholic theological schools, operating with a shortage of clergy, are already shifting in this direction. Increasing numbers of Catholic lay persons are studying theology and entering the church's deaconate. Lay theologians have been a tradition among Eastern Orthodox Christians. Among Protestant mainline churches and others there has been an increase in the number of "Commissioned Lay Pastors." Denominational schools are offering basic mini-courses required for lay pastors who are selected to function in small churches that cannot afford full-time clergy. Informed laity have always known that theological education is not the sole possession of the clergy. How receptive are theological schools of all traditions to receiving qualified laity to study alongside seminarians? Are theological schools willing to allocate scarce resources to support the laity in their studies? Without providing tangible signs of support, schools will limit the opportunities for laity to be theological partners with the clergy. We should, I believe, establish scholarship programs for the laity as we do for seminarians so that the people of God might witness together more knowledgably in the public square.

Loren Mead, founder of the Alban Institute, has a point when he observes that:

> The relationship between clergy and the laity over the years has built chronic overfunctioning into the role of the clergy and underfunctioning into the role of the laity. The clergy have come to expect the laity to under-function and the prophecy is self-fulfilling. The laity has come to expect the clergy to overfunction, and this, too, is self-fulfilling. Neither finds it easy to challenge the depressingly self-replicating pattern of dependence.[2]

In time, we will see a "lay paradigm" co-existing in theological schools with a "clergy paradigm," both enjoying support as the people of God together confront the challenges of the twenty-first century.[3]

## Using Retired Theological Educators

To address the expanding demand for theological education by God's people in their faith journeys, we will need to organize and deploy more intentionally than we have the services and talents of retired theological educators. For this purpose, accredited theological schools might consider supporting the creation of a national academy of retired theological educators in collaboration with ATS.

According to *Auburn Studies*, of the ATS accredited schools representing some 243 institutions, as many as two-thirds of their theological faculties have retired or will retire between the years 1991 and 2006.[4] This is not to mention the unknown number of full-time administrators who will also depart, largely due to retirement. There is a graying of leadership in theological education in North America, a factor that calls for discussion and creative action as we assess the current status and continuing efforts for renewal in our theological institutions.

With the lifting of mandatory retirement in higher education and the simultaneous shrinking of churches, we have created extraordinary pressure upon theological schools to renew themselves and justify their rising costs. The situation is further compounded by the large number of younger scholars (more diversified in composition than the older generations of scholars) seeking to enter the job market, but discovering that there is no predictable retirement pattern of senior scholars.

There are a variety of reasons why eligible persons no longer wish to retire at the actuarial benchmark of "sixty-five." Many are fulfilled in what they are doing. In many aspects, this is a blessing, since the school benefits from the continued service of outstanding senior scholars. However, the health of an organization, and especially educational institutions, calls also for an intergenerational faculty and staff.

What we recognized on our campus, once we addressed the financial and benefit needs confronting persons approaching retirement, was the more difficult question of personal identity. What is missing for many after retirement, I feel, is the opportunity for wider service and peer relationships that an Academy of Retired Theological Educators could provide. Many theological educators remain committed to meaningful service after retirement. Many wish to continue teaching, writing, consulting, and researching in their chosen area. Retirement liberates them from institutional obligations and cares, allowing them to pursue special projects. Nonetheless, the need for camaraderie and continued service remains strong.

An Academy of Retired Theological Educators would provide a vehicle for retirees to be connected to a world of opportunities for service at home and abroad, through schools, churches, social government agencies, etc. It could be modeled after the International Executive Corporation, founded in 1964, which has completed well over 16,000 advisory projects in more than 129 countries. Pittsburgh Seminary has been the beneficiary of several retired executives in our business and development offices; having volunteers is an aspect of creative budgeting at the seminary that we value.

While various "Volunteers in Mission" programs are maintained under the auspices of several denominations, the specific aim of an Academy of Retired Theological Educators would be to provide a clearinghouse for those who could serve as theologians in residence to local churches, act as advisors, or become adjunct faculty in numerous settings, and share their organizing, writing, and fund-raising skills.

Perhaps the ATS or its designee would act as the administrative agent to maintain such an Academy. The possibilities can be explored through an initial planning grant from foundations interested in linking theological education to churches and mission institutions. The intention is to keep the structure of the Academy as simple as possible and free from bureaucratic entrapments. It should function as a catalyst of the Spirit to further personal and institutional renewal for all who participate. The creation of such an Academy, I believe, would supply an important piece in the renewing of theological education and its widening service in North America and beyond.

## The Church as Seminary
## and the Seminary as Church

In spite of all these endeavors to extend theological education among the churches, we will still have failed if we do not recognize that churches and theological schools are actually engaged in a common pursuit—namely, to discover the divine will for our lives and to be guided by divine wisdom in our life together. As the people of God, we never cease in our pursuit of God's will and wisdom for our lives, for we know in our hearts that herein lies our fulfillment and destiny. Seminarians and parishioners participate in a common quest; neither is more holy or worthy than the other; together we are placed in God's "hothouse"—God's seminary, if you will—to nurture and strengthen us to fulfill a divine destiny yet unknown to us, but which promises to be a journey far beyond our imagination.

While the psalmist informs us that the earth belongs to God and the heavens as well (Psalm 121), within these perimeters we are pilgrims—seminarians and parishioners are students together on a faith journey of learning driven by our questions rather than the answers we have. The purpose of theological education is to assist us in asking the right questions and allow us to recognize and be dissatisfied with poor answers, inviting the Spirit of God always to be our eternal compass. Theological schools are at best imperfect beacons in this journey, guiding us to safe harbors, sanctuaries of rest and renewal in our pilgrimage of faith. We will discover as we are led that there is a creative synergy between seminaries and churches. In their mutual interdependence, churches can become seminaries and seminaries can become churches, each discovering the limits of our finiteness before the majesty and mystery of God.

Churches can become more seminary-like through the following means:

1. *Discipline.* Membership standards are generally slack in our churches and the faithful core is diminishing. In the early years of Christianity, it took at least three years of disciplined faithfulness to be admitted to the household of faith. Today, we have reversed the process—it normally takes three years of graduate study to become an ordained pastor, while anyone it seems can easily become a member of a congregation. A disciplined membership process at the grassroots must be reintroduced if the church is to become more like a seminary. "But the church can't be like a seminary," protested a pastor to me one day. "We simply don't have the same control as you do. We don't give grades. For us, pass/fail grades are left to God." But sooner or later we will all realize that we can't share an authentic and informed faith without discipline, which sets a tone and presents an example of commitment to inquirers. Seeking God's will and wisdom calls us to obedience and discipline in the process.

2. *Study.* Study of God's Word should be at the heart of our activities and worship services in the church. An uninformed congregation cannot carry out the church's mission. The church as seminary should regularly sponsor rigorous Bible study courses that meaningfully integrate theological, ethical, and pastoral concerns, clarifying the church's tradition and expanding its outreach. Perhaps a theologian-in-residence program could be instituted with one or more churches cooperating and inviting a faculty member on sabbatical or a retired theological educator to offer classes.

3. *Prayer.* What many refer to as spiritual formation in our theological seminaries should also become an essential emphasis in the local church. The church as seminary must not only promote prayer among parishioners, but also assist believers to have a prayerful style of living. Our goal should be a life of constant communication with God, a state of mind that calls for a praying attitude in the midst of our activities and anxieties.

4. *Engagement.* The best learning takes place through engagement. Too much preaching leads to passivity, as does too much lecturing. The church as a seminary must find ways for parishioners to express and demonstrate their discipleship through relationships, advocacy opportunities, and numerous other means of social and community involvement.

Similarly, *churches can encourage seminaries to become more like churches.* Discipline, study, prayer, and engagement are necessary for the local congregation, but also for our seminaries. Churches can help seminaries to be more vital in four ways:

1. The local congregation by example can assist the seminary to balance criticism with charity. The church is often more accepting of people's frailties than are seminary student bodies and faculties.
2. The practice of forgiveness at the grassroots must also be witnessed in the seminary classroom. Forgiveness ought to be more than a discussion topic between instructor and student.
3. The local church can teach the seminary the cost of discipleship. During our seminary years, we become conditioned to receiving, and at times not enough genuine sharing takes place. Basic to any sharing is the need to listen and hear one another's concerns. Seminaries and seminarians must also share materially in the church's mission, no matter how limited our resources. A small contribution for the hungry and oppressed in the world from a seminarian's meager budget or a generous sharing of time and talents is meaningful discipleship. Only through genuine giving of self and substance can we establish community. Retired church members who have volunteered to contribute their services to our seminaries have taught us that true community is not created by what we get, but rather by what we give.
4. There is oftentimes greater tolerance for diversity in our local churches than we have manifested in seminary communities. In our seminaries, we utter considerable lip service to diversity, while seeking conformity to the prevailing ethos on campus. Seminarians play games to test one another's standard of orthodoxy. We need to move beyond such testing and learn to see others without labels, discovering the authenticity of each person's faith witness. Field education plays a key role as it offers students a glimpse of the local church at its best and at its worst. Through proper guidance, these field-based experiences are among the most important "seminary classrooms" for demonstrating at times loving acceptance in the midst of diversity.

Neither the seminary nor the church has lived up to its potential. The mandate is clear for the people of God: churches can learn from seminaries and seminaries from churches, each acquiring from the other what it lacks. Only through mutual exchange can we hope to uphold "the priesthood of all believers," called as we are not only to proclaim but also to practice our faith (James 2:14–36).

## Theological Education in the Digital Age

The greatest horizon for the expansion of seminary education and the church's outreach may lie with the seemingly limitless potential of the Internet. We are in the early stages of the Digital Age; institutions and individuals are now learning quickly what *being digital*[5] means. In part, it is about a new way of living that ushers us into a world becoming more decentralized, globalized, harmonized, and empowering for humankind.[6] Being digital implies the permission to exercise our capacity to grow into this new style of life.

The new technology is transforming all aspects of life; the modern industrial economy has witnessed its coexistence with an emerging informational postmodern economy, call it the new *"global market culture,"* creating both harmony and dissonance at the same time. The tension is sometimes referred to as "the digital divide," separating those who feel empowered from those who feel disempowered by the new technology. It is within this new context that churches and theological schools must re-think how we will deliver our message of timeless and transcendent hope. How can we use the new technology to teach and proclaim our message without turning ourselves into technocrats? It is with an attitude of cautious exploration that we approach the Net and its future implications for theological education.

While I do not concur completely with Professor David E. Noble of York University in Toronto, Canada, who claims that "distance education is fool's gold,"[7] his comments do cause us to pause and review our uses of the new technology. Noble sees the craze for online education as a profit-making venture on the part of corporations rather than sound pedagogy. He also believes that the rights of professors in cyberspace will be violated, our privacy taken away, our materials stolen, and jobs lost. Noble wishes to challenge the growing expectation of salvation through technology and the turning of higher education into "Digital Diploma Mills."[8] That doesn't mean that he doesn't see the benefits of education through the Internet for those who are stationed in remote spots unable to pursue other educational options, but that he believes these benefits shouldn't be driving the academic agenda as they have. Noble believes the whole matter should be placed in a more limited perspective, as was distance education through correspondence courses in an earlier day. None of these distance forms of education is a substitute, according to Noble, for the "old-fashioned, low-tech classroom" seen as "sacred space."[9] But why does Noble see the issue of technology in such either/or terms? The Gutenberg and post-Gutenberg eras can coexist, I believe, as we seek to nurture the people of God with a combination of options that fulfill both residential and non-residential requirements among theological schools without becoming "Digital Diploma Mills."

The ATS is seeking to steer its member schools along a similar path with its recent standards that limit the number of credits that can be earned through distance education.[10] There is no doubt that the "old-fashioned" interface between instructors and students can be enhanced through technology. The

Net enables an extended community to become learners, which is not really possible if we limit ourselves to the traditional on-campus residential programs. We might even discover that the new technical tools for teaching along with older methods together can make a potent combination to the benefit of students and faculty. It will certainly extend the geographic outreach of our schools as well as include us within a global community of theological students, faculty, and laity.

I believe theological schools can learn from the advancements already made in distance education. For instance, after five years of planning, the Association Colleges of the South are offering a "virtual classics department" of six professors from six colleges with thirty-six students. The professors will teach an advanced Latin course together, combining high tech means with face-to-face discussions on each of the individual liberal arts campuses. Other forms of collaboration are being explored through Project 2001, a partnership of sixty-two liberal arts colleges working to enhance learning through technology with modern language instruction for their students. "The arrangement will let students on each campus have the close contact with a professor, an attractive aspect of liberal arts colleges. But the student will also get to communicate with students and professors at a distance."[11] We can also learn from graduate professional schools in law, medicine, and business, in their efforts with online courses and continuing education events as we rethink our current levels of involvement with the Internet.

Theological schools can also team-teach on the Internet. The collaboration would be an exciting learning venture for faculties as well as for students.[12] Just think of the limitless possibilities that exist for theological schools if ecumenical team-taught courses could be designed for continuing education events and credit courses for seminarians, clergy, and laity. I believe that digital technology can work synergistically with the best modes of traditional teaching to offer us stimulating and meaningful learning experiences from both worlds.[13] The Digital Age provides a powerful means to unite the people of God as never before in becoming the Body of Christ, "worshipping, learning, and living out the good news of John 3:16 within the world."[14] The horizons for seminary education are unlimited as we learn from the pioneering attempts of other colleagues in higher education.

### DISCUSSION STARTER

*I*n what ways would you further expand the horizon of theological education at your school? Are the possibilities discussed in this chapter diluting the traditional mission of our schools? If we continue to operate within the prevailing "clerical paradigm," will we miss an opportunity to be of greater service to the churches? If we pursue a "people of God paradigm," I suspect that we will soon discover that our present resources are insufficient, but at the same time, we will have a more compelling case to make before the churches and the public for their support in expanding theological education. Do you concur? If not, why not?

# PART III  Student Concerns

Chapter 9

# Who Is Qualified to Minister?

### Today's Theological Student

Seminarians and divinity students perpetually worry about whether they are truly called to ministry. Admissions committees wish to have candidates who possess the intelligence, creativity, commitment, and caring spirit necessary to lead churches struggling in a changing society. The affirmation that students and schools seek is unfortunately not always evident to either party. Choosing future ministers is not a perfect science.

I believe that we are not attracting sufficient numbers of candidates for the clergy with the capacity to lead and transform churches and church-related institutions. Is this a result of the general malaise and decline among churches? Barbara Wheeler, President of the Auburn Seminary and Center for the Study of Theological Education conducted a recent study of student profiles; she challenges theological schools to raise the admissions bar.[1] In spite of the recurring financial worries that preoccupy many theological schools, the enlistment of qualified candidates for ministry, I believe, is the single most important issue confronting theological schools now and into the foreseeable future.[2]

In 1998, the Auburn Center conducted a survey for the Fund for Theological Education to determine a profile of Master's level students entering seminary in September 1998, based on 159 schools of the ATS that chose to participate with a 24.8 percent return.[3] Highlights of the survey findings indicate that while 80 percent of the incoming students say their goal is a "religious" profession or occupation, only 60 percent plan to be ordained. This fact isn't so alarming if we choose to operate under a "people of God" paradigm rather than a "clerical" paradigm; what should concern us is that among seminarians at the ATS schools entering the 1998 class, the goal of less than one-third of the students under the age of thirty is directed to congregational or parish ministry. These numbers will not satisfy the present or future clergy needs of our churches. It should also be noted that another segment of the

81

surveyed students, more than one-quarter, indicated their wish to enter institutional chaplaincies in hospitals, prisons, the military, and campus ministries.

According to the survey, the majority of entering students in 1998 did not have a humanities major in their undergraduate background, nor the prerequisites in philosophy, literature, and history that would be helpful. Today, students come from a wide assortment of undergraduate and graduate programs. In addition, students entering theological schools are older and at times rusty in their study habits. Faculties in turn are reluctantly shifting their expectation from the liberal arts student to the "street smart" second-career students.[4] Intentional efforts are being made by some theological schools to attract younger students of promise through such programs as our seminary's Summer Youth Institute for rising high school seniors who show promise for leadership and have been nominated by their pastors as a potential leader for the church.

According to the survey, most theological schools make significant efforts to recruit women and minority students. Women currently make up one-third of the entering student body and number as many as one-half or more in some schools. This corresponds to what is happening in other professional schools such as law and medicine. But students in those professional schools tend to be younger than those coming to theological schools. Our racial and ethnic representations tend to parallel other professional schools, but African Americans and Hispanics continue to be underrepresented compared to their percentages in the general population. Some of this is due to the greater financial disadvantage that many African Americans, Asians, and Hispanics have had. Theological schools are always working to remove such financial barriers.

Included below is a summary of the responses to the Auburn Center questionnaire:[5]

# A SURVEY SNAPSHOT

For the *Survey of Master's Level Students Entering Seminary in September 1998*, FTE asked the Auburn Center to pay close attention to what younger students—those under thirty—had to say in comparison with older students.* What did we learn? Here is a snapshot:

Average age of entering seminarians
    All students: 35.0
    Women: 36.9
    Men: 34.1
    Evangelical Protestants: 32.3
    Mainline Protestants: 36.8
    Roman Catholics: 38.7

Activities before seminary
    Very active in worship
        Younger students: 53%
        Older students: 73%

Leadership in campus religious organizations
    Younger students: 45%
    Older students: 20%

Areas of undergraduate study
    Humanities/religion/philosophy
    Younger students: 48%
    Older students: 33%

    Social science/education/fine arts
    Younger students: 32%
    Older students: 33%

    Science/math/technical studies
    Younger students: 20%
    Older students: 34%

**Motives for seeking theology degree (1=not important 2=somewhat important 3=important 4=very important)**

Sense of call
    Younger students: 3.62
    Older students: 3.75

Desire to lead worship
    Younger students: 2.12
    Older students: 2.75

Desire to bring change to religious community
    Younger students: 2.9
    Older students: 2.6

Desire to change society
    Younger students: 2.0
    Older students: 1.8

Desire for spiritual fulfillment
    Younger students: 3.2
    Older students: 3.4

**Plans for M.Div. students**

Ordained or plan to be ordained
    Younger students: 54%
    Older students: 65%

Congregational ministry
    Younger students: 30%
    Older students: 40%

Counseling or spiritual direction
    Younger students: 8%
    Older students: 10%

Academic teaching
    Younger students: 20%
    Older students: 15%

*Some percentages are approximations.

## Leadership and the Fruit of the Spirit

The first disciples Jesus called were not graduates of a liberal arts education. Many of them could be referred to as "second-career" candidates, recruited from their fishing and tax-collecting activities. Most were probably under-educated or illiterate, but they were nevertheless intelligent, adventurous, caring, and ambitious. They were willing to risk and think "outside the box" in their spiritual quest for renewal; they were surprised and at times overjoyed with the fresh vision Jesus brought to his teaching ministry, reinforced by his acts of healing and simple lifestyle. The "academic emphasis" and passion for theological education came later, with the apostle Paul and his contemporaries in the early church.

Jesus' source of empowerment resided in his faithful relationship to God, which was manifested with the "signs of wonder" in his practice of ministry. Today, we might refer to his abilities to empower others as "the fruit of the Spirit," which includes "love, joy, peace, patience, kindness, generosity, faithfulness, gentleness, and self-control" (Galatians 5:22–23). All of these qualities can be summed up as "emotional intelligence," which is necessary for effective leadership, but is often neglected today.[6] From my faith perspective, the practice of emotional intelligence is essentially a gift of the Spirit that can only be partially learned. Emotional intelligence has to do with our sense of self-awareness that enables us to suspend judgment and to listen empathetically, without being condescending. Emotional intelligence is also the passion to work beyond personal self-gain and to possess the desire and ability to find common ground and build rapport on issues of conflict.[7] Emotional intelligence is the secular way of speaking of *soul nurturing*. It is difficult for an admission committee to uncover whether a candidate for ministry possesses this required gift for leadership in ministry. It is certainly not evident by reviewing the transcript of grades. The seminary candidate will demonstrate whether a propensity for emotional intelligence exists during his or her course of studies and supervised ministry. Such Spirit-led leadership inspires others to follow because it is soul nurturing.

The "fruit of the Spirit" points us to the inherent nature of emotional intelligence. Without practicing these attributes, we will not be able to exercise the soul leadership so desperately needed in our fragmented and lonely society, preoccupied with the superficial pursuit of health and happiness. It is imperative that we nurture not only others, but taste for ourselves the "fruit of the Spirit;" otherwise, we will be ineffective educators in a society searching vainly for fulfillment and hope.

We can no longer expect to straighten out our messy society with more of the same theology of whatever stripe, or by further analytical thinking. Our calling is to venture more deeply inward to the soul, the very essence of our being, and trust the Spirit to give us a taste of "the fruit of the Spirit" that is so needed in our churches and religious institutions today. Are we willing to balance our efforts at reasoning with emotional intelligence? Or are we still bent on thinking our way out of all our problems? We ignore the fact that the very issues that divide us are irrational, revealing the darker side of our suspicious nature. Exercising soul leadership embedded in the "fruit of the Spirit" will give us a fresher perspective in tackling our problems. To become nurturing soul leaders ought to be our highest calling in ministry if we seek to serve God with greater fulfillment in the years ahead. Potential candidates seeking admission should wisely seek the gift of emotional intelligence in order to become inspired leaders for our churches and communities.

## Am I Called?

I believe the answer to the question of call is shaped by each person's unique journey of faith. The call of God is subject to a divine agenda that may not be fully disclosed at any given time. We must review our understanding of God's will regularly, for the call can zig and zag throughout our lifetime. A divine call is dynamic, not static. In retrospect, we might see a divine plan unfolding in small ways, witnessing to God's abiding faithfulness (covenant) with us, so that we might view our entire life as a calling.

In the Reformed tradition, every believer has a calling in life to minister, not just the clergy. This is why we often say to a congregation that all God's people are ministers. This concept is often referred to as "the priesthood of all believers." I believe that this "people of God" paradigm, with its emphasis on everyone's "priesthood," needs to be more widely communicated and accepted, for it has important implications for theological education which unfortunately has been largely limited to a "clerical" paradigm. Our daily task within the household of faith is to affirm each person's ministry when appropriate and to raise questions when necessary. As many of us have already discovered, we can slip easily into an uncritical stance, confusing our will with God's will, and then "baptizing" the former with God's seal of approval. This is why we in seminary admissions need careful counsel and wisdom from the church's elders as we seek to discern God's Spirit to determine who is qualified to serve in leadership roles in the church.

The decision to become a pastor involves not only self-appraisal, but also a confirmation by the church that one's particular gifts are needed to make a difference in the church's future. This is why seminaries are dependent upon congregations, college chaplains, and pastors to identify potential candidates.

The calling process informs, nurtures, and guides every individual who desires to do God's will. Let us not forget that every call is unique before God. Discovering God's call then is far more than logical thinking or an exact science, but neither is it solely subjective, limited to an individual's whim or prompted by a "push" from a zealous pastor, friend, or parent. Many may consider joining the ranks of clergy, but in actuality, only the few who truly believe they are called should enter.

Whether there is a clergy shortage or surplus isn't really the important thing; the unvarnished reality is that there is never a sufficient number of candidates who are truly gifted and feel the Spirit's voice urging them to accept God's call for a wider range of ministries serving the church and society. Everyone is called to ministry, but we are not all called to the same task. There are many endeavors where a faithful witness is needed. This fact is at times difficult to admit among theological educators themselves, who might spot a potential candidate who is headed for another vocation under God.

At the heart of everyone's self-examination of their call and qualifications for ministry lie some hidden questions: "Am I trapped in a call that is no longer fulfilling? Does God still want me to continue in this present ministry?" There are many ways to test these questions through study, reflection, discussions among peers and friends, and above all in prayerful retreat with scripture and a trusted spiritual director. I have no doubt God's will unfolds for most of us in small ways; the divine way often defies human logic and even common sense. We will discover, if we haven't already, that there are no ready blueprints in front of us, only the fact in retrospect that God's design is unfolding in bits and pieces, revealing a divine pattern for our lives, even when we feel abandoned at times. God will honor our faithfulness and guide us by a heavenly light, even when we are walking through dark shadows.

Finally, everyone called to ministry has a story to tell. Is my story or yours typical? I don't know and I don't consider the question important. Experiences vary. Yet, we all share a common core commitment or vision before God. Some accounts are dramatic while others are calmly predictable. I know pastors who haven't even articulated the path of their specific calling, but subsequent events in their lives affirm their decision to be in the ministry of Word and Sacrament. Any pilgrimage of faith involves an honest and prayerful assessment of one's self followed by a quiet period of gestation as God's will unfolds.

## The Lessons of Seminary

There are many lessons to be learned at seminary. Let me confess that I naively didn't know what to expect when I first went to seminary; but I soon discovered that, first, it was an imperfect community of persons without halos. It consisted of imperfect professors, imperfect students, imperfect administrators and staff, all of whom made imperfect decisions. It soon became clear to me that it would be impossible to love and accept one another without the practice of forgiveness, if we were to enjoy the Christian fellowship we were being taught to nurture within our future congregations.[8]

Second, the disciplines of the seminary curriculum often left us with more questions than answers. The function of theological education, I learned, was not simply to pass on information, but to make us painfully aware of the gaps existing in our quest to know; it was evident that our intellectual curiosity would never be fully satisfied. We were reminded of the fact that we walk by faith; the facts of our faith to some extent will always be incomplete.

Third, the bottom line of seminary education for me was the realization that we live our lives from grace to grace; any other life orientation is superficial by comparison. The foundational sacrament of life is God's grace, which in turn enables us to celebrate the gifts of creation, birth, and re-birth in Jesus Christ. Is there any other certitude more important than declaring our dependency upon God's grace?

Fourth, seminary education provided me with a profound respect for human finiteness. While scripture is our authoritative guide in matters of faith and doctrine, we cannot overlook the fact that scripture and the early ecumenical councils, creeds, and confessions of the church are also interpretations to our understanding and reverence for the mystery of the triune God whom we confess as Father, Son, and Holy Spirit, and as our Creator, Redeemer, and Sustainer. When all is said and written, however, we must let God be God who cannot be equated or limited to our theologies.

Fifth, seminary education encouraged me to think theologically; that is to say, to reflect on the significance and implications of heavenly intervention in human history and how we witness to this revelation within the life and worship of the church. In the course of our theological reflections, we discovered the church to be the people of God, persons who are able to apply their Christian faith meaningfully and creatively throughout the marketplace.

Sixth, seminary education introduced me to the reality and benefits of networking among future colleagues in ministry. Professional networking begun in seminary can provide a lifetime of support and friendships. Seminary is the place to discover our unity in diversity within the Body of Christ. Such a vision of unity challenges us to work for a common language of discourse within the church and society, especially as we seek to establish some agreement on moral priorities. There really cannot be any ordering of moral priorities without a language of common discourse. Seminarians who have experienced a mutual bonding on campus can model for their local communities the benefits of holding honest dialogue and reaching common moral priorities. Such an achievement will promote unity with diversity based upon trust.

Seventh, seminary is where we fashion a realistic model for ministry. Many options for ministry will be discussed in the course of one's seminary education and through this means, each of us can fashion the style of ministry that we wish to pursue. For instance, there is a great deal of talk in seminary circles on the merits of pastoral ministry versus specialized ministries. Seminaries provide opportunities to look at these options and offer situations to experiment with the various styles of leadership practiced in ministry. Hopefully, we will fashion a model for ourselves that will have a positive impact on society.

Eighth and last, I learned that seminary isn't primarily a training center or professional school; instead, it is an academy of Christian learners committed to deepening both their understanding and communication of the faith. While there is also an emphasis in the seminary's program to acquire skills in preaching and pastoral care, as well as lessons in stewardship, evangelism, administration, and conflict resolution, the weight of the curriculum falls on learning the *content* of our faith (Bible, theology, and church history), and sensitivity to the cultural *context* in which we practice our faith. Acquiring this knowledge is done from an ecclesial perspective and also includes an ecumenical and global outlook. For me, seminary education was a memorable point of embarkation into my ministry.

### DISCUSSION STARTER

Would you agree that the admission of qualified candidates for ministry should be the chief concern of theological schools for the foreseeable future? Would community life on our campuses be happier if we could demonstrate greater emotional intelligence among ourselves? No doubt conflicts in our churches could also find greater possibility for resolution if emotional intelligence were more widely practiced.

Do you see the call to ministry as a perpetual and changing call that can take us in different directions during the course of our lifetime? In other words, can God call someone to pastoral ministry and then later call someone out of pastoral ministry into a secular field? Is such switching of calls a spiritual cover-up for our earlier inadequacy? Does our piety sometimes undermine our understanding of a "call," thus preventing us from being honest with ourselves and God? Can faculty assist students at this point or are faculty and administrators themselves caught up in their own games of deception?

Were your expectations in seminary fulfilled? What would you suggest to faculty and administrators who desire to make your "seminary experience" more rewarding than it may have been for them? Are your suggestions feasible in the light of your knowledge of seminary culture? To what extent are one's disappointments with seminary or divinity school parallel to our disappointments with congregational life? To what extent have we been part of the problem rather than part of the solution in encouraging students or classmates to remain in or leave school?

Chapter 10

# Going through Seminary
# without Losing Your Faith

*T*he other day, Jane dropped by the office for a chat. Jane is a senior at the seminary where I teach—a good student, the kind of person who contributes to an instructor's own growth. I was glad to see her walk in. "What's on your mind?" I asked. Jane slumped into the easy chair and unfolded to me her increasing doubts about her Christian beliefs. "I'm losing my faith!" she cried out half-despairingly. Jane, of course, is not alone. Any number of seminarians reach their senior year harboring doubts which they reveal neither to fellow students nor to faculty.

The feeling that one is losing one's faith even while studying its sacred materials has always been a hazard of preparation for the professional ministry. Like those of yesteryear, seminarians of today are also confronted by the question, "What do I really believe?" One goal of seminary education is to assist in answering that question. The responsibility of the faculty is not to undermine faith, but to help students identify, articulate, and nurture a living faith.

### Separating Faith from Theology

During my nearly four decades of seminary teaching, each year's entering class has varied in all respects save one; namely, the large number who repeatedly have made no distinction between faith and theology. Such is the confusion that more than one student beginning his or her final year suddenly realizes that they have refused an education while trying to protect their faith. Going through seminary without learning seems to be the hidden desire of some. Students who are actually afraid that the seminary process (a necessary means to obtain one's union card) will undermine their "faith." Not infrequently a student will confide to me that a pastoral friend, a grandfather, or a saintly mother warned the student on parting: "Now don't you let that seminary take away your faith!" That type of advice is likely to make the candidate suspicious of the seminary and its faculty. I have often seen seminarians defying the professor, as it were, to take away their "faith." They mean to protect and keep alive the "faith" they brought from home. Unless each becomes aware of this fear, the instructor and the student can spend a whole semester bypassing each other amid showers of verbiage. Obviously, the instructor ought first to set about helping the defiant student to identify and analyze that "faith."

Also the faculty member is encouraged to listen attentively when students share their faith with cohorts in the classroom, for such informal "confessions" and reactions reveal much about each student's thoughts and feelings. Then, slowly, faculty will see clenched fists relaxing into open palms, signifying a spirit more receptive to learning. Once thus relaxed, students can begin to appraise the sources that have hitherto nurtured their faith. Without denying the vitality of his or her previous experiences or betraying the trust placed in them by others, the student embarks on the long but exciting process of identifying the Source beyond the sources. This is theologizing, the heart of the theological enterprise. In this way, a bridge of understanding will be built, across which dialogue will be fruitful for both student and instructor and in the process a vital faith, a radical faith, will be communicated.

For true faith is radical. Seminarians can feel that they are losing "faith." When their sense of loss becomes most pronounced, they are yearning for the comfortable past. In time, however, pilgrim seminarians begin to realize that they are called to come to God standing up straight. That is so radical a call that they may refuse to heed it and look about frantically for some theological messiah to pull them through, only to discover how humanly limited all theological messiahs are. Eventually, they face the fact that there is really no escape from the radicalness of faith. God wants us to come without help of any kind. God alone is the Source worthy of our full commitment. "I am who I am. . . . There is no other" (Exodus 3:14 and Isaiah 45:22).

Until this claim is firmly fixed in our hearts as well as our heads, we shall go on losing our "faith." Wherever there is rigorous questioning of our religious assumptions, seminary education will enable students to affirm as well as shed theologies in order to gain living faith in the Source. Philosopher Alfred North Whitehead defined religion as the denunciation of gods and also believed that religions committed suicide when they extracted their inspirations from their dogmas. This holds true in Christianity.[1] The seminary that is negligent in questioning the theological gods of our culture is shirking its responsibility to identify, articulate, and nurture faith in the living God.

## God behind Our Theologies

But isn't this faith in the living God also a theology which must be questioned? Can we have a faith without theology? According to theologian Schubert

Ogden, "faith without theology is not really faith at all; theology without faith is still theology, and quite possibly good theology at that."[2] In other words, theology is a responsible intellectual enterprise that need not presuppose faith; and faith in the living God is not necessary for theological discussion.

However, all faith statements have theological implications that are based on our spiritual experiences; and sharing these experiences always involves a tension between mystery and meaning. But in their search for meaning, seminaries often seem to relegate mystery to the sidelines. This may explain in part the neglect of spirituality in our seminaries at a time when, ironically, interest in spirituality is increasing in society. In a report on spiritual development in theological education, ATS recognizes that the "crisis of faith" among seminarians is a result of a decline in spirituality that has been going on for some years in all seminaries—liberal, conservative, independent, and denominational.[3] Obviously, a condition so widespread does not admit to any simple solution.

The tension between meaning and mystery will exist as long as the seminary is both a professional academic center and a semi-monastic center of meditation and prayer. This dual identity fits the disposition of today's seminarians who are searching for a viable mystery on which to hang their beliefs, and at the same time seeking a place in society where they might expend their energies with integrity and experience, renewing themselves and those around them. The crucial question here is whether one can educate church leaders without destroying their authentic piety. Can the tension between the search for mystery and the search for meaning be maintained?

## A Pilgrim Theology

As a learning community of faith, we must recover the biblical, radical faith that lies behind our distrust of structures, behind theological labels and their limitations. We must recapture our focus on faith as "the assurance of things hoped for, the conviction of things not seen" (Hebrews 11:1). A faith in the living God must be reasserted within our theologies. As the Russian philosopher Nicolas Berdyaev has indicated in his writings, genuine faith doesn't require theological doctrine, but it does take faith to have living beliefs. In other words, the higher priority for him is faith-generated spiritual experience over the "correctness" of doctrine. Living theology is faith based and experience based, not to be equated with the casting of faith in theological doctrines.[4] In short, spiritual experiences cannot always be explained. They are part of the unresolved tension between mystery and meaning. This is the nature of a pilgrim's theology.

Our wish to have answers for all our questions has tempted us to turn our traditional theologies into crutches. But God is beyond our grasp. Too often, the desire for an authoritative faith has led us into a rationalizing attempt to "corner" God in our respective traditions. But in every age, the reforming spirit of the church has counseled, "Let God be God." This spirit must be reaffirmed again and again, lest we be entrapped in parochialism or in the latest fad.

Again in our theologizing we must always be aware of our limitations. When all is said, God is still *incognitus, absconditus* (unknown, hidden). Only through the biblical revelation do we know of a God of grace and mercy, whom we worship in faith. For the Christian, this God is most meaningfully present to us in Jesus Christ. But God himself is unknowable, beyond our means for verification. At most, we can but hold an attitude of reverent agnosticism regarding the divine nature.

The (Eastern) Orthodox tradition has long taught that God's essence is unknown, that only the divine energies can be discerned. This teaching is reflected in Orthodoxy's method of negative (or apophatic) theologizing, as opposed to the more positive (or kataphatic) theologizing of the West. Our increasing acquaintance with Eastern Christianity will no doubt lead us to place limits on our theological conclusions.

Rather than attempt to harmonize the two, we must let God be God and Jesus be Jesus. In the spirit of the Epistle to the Hebrews, we must allow the radicalness of faith to permeate our witness as we communicate to others the simplicity of faith. Too often we theological educators sacrifice the art of being simple in our attempts to be academically more precise. We forget that our theology may be nothing more than educated ignorance at a higher level of abstraction. Through private prayer, corporate worship, and the doxology we are reminded both of the simplicity of our faith and of the fact that our theological journey in this life is never completed. Ours will always be a pilgrim theology, a theology of moving and of waiting in response to the living Lord. All the evidence is not in, and no matter how earnestly we try, the last word will be God's, not ours. This eschatological reality marks our line of accountability. Living on this side of that line should humble us to limit our claims and to remember that we speak and act always in the shadow of the Divine Presence.

It is our task, then, to question all existing theologies, prone as each is to the temptation of idolatry. So doing, we shall maintain the radicalness of our faith. H. Richard Niebuhr once observed: "Man as a practical living being never exists without a god or gods; some things there are to which he must cling as the sources and goals of his activity, the centers of value."[5] Theological education should be designed to help us distinguish among the gods, so that our faith may be solidly anchored in the living God.

I have seen many students begin their professional careers in the ministry. Hopefully, in the years when they and we, their teachers, together sought the living God behind our theologies, each one began the process to grasp the significance of separating faith from theology. To return to Jane (or was it Joe?), she was not losing her faith, but deepening it; she was discarding theological casings she had outgrown. But as she continues her pilgrimage, she will need new casings to hold the enlarging breadth and depth of her faith in the living God.

## Will the Seminary Increase Faith?

On all sides we hear the cry that we need leaders of faith in our churches and theological schools. You might well ask, "Is there any guarantee that seminary education will increase faith?" The reality is that study at a theological school will not necessarily guarantee an increase of faith to anyone. How I wish it were otherwise! We could then advertise, "ENROLL HERE; WE GRADUATE GIANTS IN THE FAITH." The curriculum that can guarantee an increase in faith, I believe, has not been discovered as yet. In fact, I would be suspicious of any theological school that made such a claim; and yet, I know those of us who are responsible for theological education do wish to graduate candidates for ministry who will become outstanding and valuable leaders of the faith.

Recently, a chairperson of a pastoral search committee called me and inquired about a candidate. He asked, "Do you know this minister well?" "Yes, I do," I replied. "Tell me," he said, "is the candidate a real believer, or simply a professional in ministry?" The chairperson was looking for a *faith-driven candidate* whom the congregation and community could recognize as a believer, backed by energy, enthusiasm, and a depth in spirituality—a closeness to God—and the ability to communicate that divine presence to others. God expects us to be believers, not simply professionals in marketing and ministry.

Let us be under no illusion. Acquiring knowledge, gathering information, going through the process of reflection and interpretation do not in themselves enhance faith. If it were so, seminary faculty members would have a distinct advantage. However, it has been my observation that earned degrees and years of experience in theological education do not necessarily increase faith.

At the same time, the church and society are out looking for authentic believers—persons whose lives reflect and demonstrate a transforming message of good news that offers hope, lifting our horizons to envision a more humane form of life where love, justice, peace, and forgiveness prevail. I suspect the largest number of authentic believers is found among the faithful laity in our churches, where their witness and acts of grace have provided healing and renewal in the lives of countless people.

Today, those of us privileged to study and work within a theological seminary must recapture a realistic view of what is needed in our churches and seminaries—a more committed discipleship through increased faith. However, I wonder who has sufficient faith to lead the way? Many of us tend to be more anxiety driven in our lives than faith driven. We circle around the promised land, but fail to claim it in faith; the Kingdom of God remains only as a lecture topic on our lips. Our personal agenda and the confusing noise of our culture have muted the still small voice, cooled our passions, and thwarted the will of God unfolding through our lives. Where is the joy and hope that stems from a vibrant faith? Are we confused in our understanding of faith?

Perhaps we need to return to basics and ask ourselves, "What is faith?" Historically in the life of the church, faith has been understood in two ways. First, it has been seen in the context of beliefs held by the church and expressed in our creeds, confessions, and dogmas. This ecclesiastical definition of faith calls for critical study and review in our classrooms. Seminary education seriously studies this heritage of faith to determine what is normative for the faithful. Scholarship provides us with insight that in turn informs and nurtures the faith imbedded in our spiritual journey. Everyone's search and pilgrimage are unique. Through seminary education, we seek to establish reliable norms as we articulate and filter the Christian faith according to our respective traditions.

The second understanding of faith is more personal and private, and assumes that everyone has a starting point in faith. Here faith is seen as more a matter of the will rather than the intellect. Faith in this context is much more than a mental assent to a body of beliefs; it represents the very foundation of a person's confidence. Faith in this context is concerned with the task of establishing trust. For the believer, faith is trust, pointing us to that dynamic I-THOU relationship, a dialogue that hopefully continues and grows daily.

The essence behind the realities of life is relationships. For the believer, the basic relationship is with God—a relationship that has been made intimate through God's activity in Christ where we experience both acceptance and forgiveness by divine grace, justified as we are by our faith, not by our achievements or status. The Reformers emphasized this meaningful dependence on the Divine as justification by faith, pointing to a gracious and loving God whose primary business is reconciliation and restoration of broken relationships. As John Calvin expressed it, "Now we shall possess a right definition of faith if we call it a firm and certain knowledge of God's benevolence towards us, founded upon the truth of the freely given promise in Christ both revealed to our minds and sealed upon our hearts through the Holy Spirit."[6]

Scripture defines the history of biblical faith succinctly in the Epistle to the Hebrews, where we read that "faith is the assurance of things hoped for, the conviction of things not seen. Indeed, by faith our ancestors received approval" (Hebrews 11:1–2). The epistle goes on to state that we are now surrounded by a cloud of giants in the faith—led by Jesus who is the pioneer and perfector of our faith and who pursued the will of God that led him to the cross. Jesus was a believer!

The church needs disciples today who are truly believers, persons who have sufficient faith and commitment to make a difference in society. We need to narrow the gap between our shallow expressions of faith and that evidenced by the founder of our faith, Jesus Christ. If seminary experiences do not necessarily increase faith, what role, then, does the seminary play in narrowing the distance between our faith and the faith of Jesus? To respond to this question on your campus, why not hold a series of town meetings, followed up by subsequent small group discussions and chat rooms, which might prove beneficial and stimulating to all the members of the seminary community.

From my perspective, the seminary ought to function as a *faith-shaping community*. The responsibility falls on each of us—faculty, students, and staff—as we contribute in our own way to the total seminary experience. That is to say, we need to pay greater attention to the *ungraded curriculum* at school, as well as our published curriculum. Many of us must enlarge our involvement in the total educational process.

The root meaning of "to educate" is not only to nurture, but to draw out. The seminary faculty's task is certainly not limited to sharing information and interpretations in classes, but also providing educational leadership in and out of the classroom that draws out and reviews the faith of each student. Likewise, the faculty members need to remind themselves that the professor is also "one who professes a faith." This explains in part why it has been a tradition in most seminary classes to begin with prayer. Faculty members are expected to have a living relationship with the Source of faith and not be afraid to share their struggles and joys if they are truly to be mentors to our seminarians.

This ungraded curriculum, sometimes referred to as a "hidden curriculum," exists in the relationships that comprise every educational institution, including seminaries. These relationships are seen in faculty committees, student association gatherings, class discussions, chapel services, meal times, socials, dorm and apartment life, small group gatherings, and among special interest groups on campus. This "hidden curriculum" influences for good or ill our life together and can be a formative force, outweighing at times the academic curriculum published in the catalog. In short, the ungraded curriculum on the seminary campus is an important means by which our faith can be enhanced or hindered for years to come. For many seminarians, the most positive memories of seminary life date back to events experienced through the "hidden curriculum."

As Jane left my office, we both knew that she was not losing her faith. Instead, her faith was undergoing a major transformation—she was about to embark from seminary with a more vital understanding of her faith, which was both exciting and challenging at the same time. The journey of faith is filled with joy, anguish, and unexpected turns, for there is no other odyssey comparable to the quest for God who captures our heart, mind, and soul in the process. This is why loving God is the foremost lesson in theological education according to Jesus (Matthew 22:36–38).

### DISCUSSION STARTER

*W*hat is your assessment of the role of the "ungraded curriculum" on your campus? Do you concur that the ungraded curriculum provides avenues for meaningful relationships where we can encourage one another's faith and spiritual growth? The seminary is probably unique among graduate schools; it is meant to be a faith-shaping community where scholarship and worship provide the unique combination for community development through relationships. Is there any other graduate school that expects its students to pray, attend chapel, and build community as part of the educational experience? The health of a seminary community resides in the quality of its spiritual life—where loving concern empowers one another, where healing encounters lead to wholeness, where forgiveness leads to peacemaking and a rediscovery of one another's humanity.

Everyone brings some faith to the seminary community; but have you discovered that some claim a monopoly on having the "right" faith? Actually, we can learn and grow through sharing together when there is a willingness to risk being open and honest with one another. This also involves our willingness to suspend judgment on one another's faith. Then and only then can we become a faith-shaping and enriching community of believers.

The responsibility rests with each of us to engage in dialogue; building community calls for an unlocking of self and a searching out to others in faith. Our relationship to God, nurtured by the seminary's ungraded curriculum, plays a decisive role toward the development of our spiritual maturity. Has this been your experience? If not, why not?

Recently, I asked a faculty member what seminary education did for him, in retrospect. My colleague replied, "Seminary education provided me with 1. information; 2. an interpretive point of view; 3. practical skills; and 4. an increased enthusiasm to be a student of scripture for life." "And did your seminary experience increase your faith?" I asked. "Yes," he responded. "In seminary, I caught an excitement for my faith from one of my professors, who turned the classroom into a community, giving me and others a vision, as well as a relationship, that has inspired me throughout my lifetime." Here is an example where the graded and ungraded aspects of seminary life converged successfully, mutually enriching faith and understanding. The learning process neither begins nor ends at the door of the seminary classroom. Our faith is nurtured through meaningful relationships whenever we choose to initiate genuine dialogue. Do we understand the nature of true dialogue? How many of us have witnessed authentic dialogue that increases faith?

Chapter 11

# The Place of Prayer in Seminary Education

*P*rayer is at the heart of theological education. The quality of our prayer life measures the progress of our faith journey. Theological education provides perspective and substance to our prayers; but there is no guarantee that "educated prayers" are more effective than the prayers of a novice. As a learning community in theological studies, we must always bear this in mind. During seminary years, we often subordinate the development of our prayer life to the information and stimulation provided in our courses. We may know that there is no need for division between prayer life and intellectual pursuits; however, when we analyze where we spend most of our time, the classroom and the library often overshadow the chapel.

### Where Is Theology Practiced?

There may be a "chapel" vs. "classroom" struggle for some members of seminary communities, who have yet to integrate these two experiences harmoniously. Consequently, some theological campuses are no longer communities of expectation. Prayer life has become sterile. We are too busily engaged in cognitive learning, neglecting the spiritual dimension to complement our intellectual pursuits. The educational agenda of our theological schools is not yet sufficiently holistic. For the most part, it seems we have left spirituality to outsiders and para-church movements.

Some time ago, I asked a seminary classmate if the understanding of prayer he brought to seminary and his present understanding of prayer were different. His immediate response was, "Yes." His understanding of prayer, he said, had benefited from thirty-six years of experience. "And what does this mean?" I asked. His response was less clear at this point. "I guess," he said, "prayer is an expression of my private, personal struggle to gain a greater grasp on the meaning of life. Prayer enables me to be open with God; it is an expression of my ongoing trust in God." "But were you less trusting," I asked, "less open earlier in your life when you accepted your call to ministry?" I felt

I had been unfair in pressing for further clarity in what was obviously an ambiguous situation for him. I wonder what progress any of us have made in our prayer life since our pilgrimage of faith began. If we would confess to one another, we might admit that we have even regressed, or that at best our journey of faith reveals a zigzag pattern and little progress.

Many within our seminary communities are in a better position today to articulate their struggles with God than when they first entered our hallowed halls. After all, the theological community is where exegesis takes place—we exegete not only the scriptural text and context, but also our range of experiences—learning to place tragedies as well as joys within perspective. Prayer for many of us is a means of reviewing the text and context of our experiences in dialogue with God. Theological schools are indeed appropriate places to practice the hermeneutics of prayer.

To pray is to engage simultaneously in many aspects of dialogue with God—at one moment we are expressing adoration and praise, in another thanksgiving and confession, announcing our sorrows as well as blessings, and presenting further petitions and supplications before God. All prayers are premised on God's grace and freedom to respond to us. The believer trusts that God has our best interest at heart; it is for this reason that every prayer is uttered in the spirit that God's will, not ours, be done. The Psalms and Lord's Prayer are our models for praying.

Eugene H. Peterson, well-known writer and translator of scripture, informs us that "the impulse to pray is deep within us, at the very center of our created being, and so practically anything will do to get us started—'Help' and 'Thanks!' are our basic prayers."[1] Frankly, there is no "insider" language to prayer. "Prayer," he points out, "is elemental, not advanced, language. It is the means by which our language becomes honest, true, and personal in response to God. It is the means by which we get everything in our lives in the open before God."[2]

It's not surprising then that we have the Pauline admonition to "pray without ceasing" (1 Thessalonians 5:17). On our seminary campus, the presence of a twenty-four hour prayer room, regular chapel services, and prayers before classes, at times in faculty and administrative offices, and at the beginning and close of committee meetings, are ways in which institutionally we attempt to follow through on the apostolic admonition to "pray without ceasing." On a personal level, we are tempted to ignore this praying attitude toward life; we are too busy trying to make it on our own. Even as we study the sacred subjects of the curriculum, including classes on spirituality, we know there is a gap between where we are and where we need to be in our communion with God.

## Learning to Pray and Study "without Ceasing"

To say that prayer is at the heart of theological education is to emphasize that we need prayer institutionally and individually. To pray "without ceasing" is both an activity and a state of being that engages our hearts, minds, and souls. Within such a composite outlook, we can foster an atmosphere of expectation and excitement to energize our studies and community life together. We must learn to pray with our eyes open as well as shut: open to the facts and insights nurtured in our classrooms, and shut in meditation and wonder before the mysteries of God that defy absolute definition.

John Calvin often referred to the world around us as a "theater of God's glory." To transform this world into the Kingdom of God calls for praying with our eyes open as well as with our eyes shut. In Christian history, there are two traditions of prayer and theologizing: apophatic and kataphatic. Apophatic prayer is "praying with eyes shut," centering on the divine in silence, knowing that all human expressions of conceptualizing are inadequate. Kataphatic prayer is "praying with eyes open," seeking to express in a limited way the majesty of divine grace experienced. Both approaches at their deepest levels view prayer as listening for God's peace and presence, beyond words and images as we enter into a unifying moment of ecstasy and tranquility.[3] Being at one with God (John 17) and listening to the murmuring of the Spirit within the silence of our hearts are the essence of prayer.

Praying is a universal exercise among all religionists of every persuasion. Every tradition in its own way fights against turning prayers into forms without substance. The late, distinguished Rabbi Abraham Joshua Heschel has implied in his writing that seeking God in our theologizing is more than a matter of information; it is actually a matter of prayer. Our journey is to get close to God: "it involves a desire for experience rather than a search for information. . . . Indeed, to pray does not only mean to seek *help*, it also means to seek *Him*."[4] For Heschel, talking *about* God, which is what theological educators do, can become idle chatter unless one first learns to talk *to* God. Prayer "does not have to be always on our lips; it must always be on our minds, in our hearts."[5] Real prayer then seeks to address God through awe and silence, not chatter.

Unless we dialogue prayerfully with God, the academic study of theology can indeed become arid. Prayer needs to be foundational to all theological education if the excitement and enthusiasm for studying the sacred is to flourish. William James has rightly said, "Prayer is the very soul and essence of religion."[6] Prayer is the religious experience *par excellence* that is available to each of us. Prayer is much more than the human attempt to bend God's will to our will. Prayer is more than the human manipulation of divine provi-dence—a form of spiritual lobbying for our desires. Prayer instead quickens our sense of social responsibility and stewardship before God. Without fear, we ask for God's will to be done in our lives, believing in a loving and gra-cious God.

What we pray for and what we theologize about are closely interrelated. This is why theologian George S. Henry used a simple device in forming a judgment on the writings of theologians past and present. He looked for what the theologian said about prayer. If a theologian took prayer seriously, Henry took the theologian seriously. For Henry realized that prayer is the funda-mental way we relate to God. Prayer is our way of expressing trust in God, finding affirmation as we move closer to the divine purpose and meaning in our lives. Augustine rightly acknowledged that we are restless until we find our rest in God.[7]

### The Relevance of Prayer
### in Keeping Us Connected

Prayer is also our means to combat the demons and dinosaurs in our midst. Karl Barth, in his insightful book entitled *Prayer*, uncovers from Luther's *Large Catechism* the idea that prayer is necessary in our demonic struggles. According to Luther, "We know that our defense lies in prayer alone. We are too weak to resist the Devil and his vassals. Let us hold fast to the weapons of the Christian; they enable us to combat the Devil. For what has carried off these great victories over the undertakings of our enemies which the Devil has used to put us in subjection, if not the prayers of certain pious people who rose up as a rampart to protect us? Our enemies may mock at us. But we shall oppose both them and the Devil if we maintain ourselves in prayer and if we persist in it. For we know that when a Christian prays in this way: 'Dear Father, thy will be done,' God replies to him, 'Dear child, yes, it shall be done in spite of the Devil and of the whole world.' "[8]

In the desert, Jesus also used prayer to counter Satan. He was tempted fol-lowing his forty days of fasting in the wilderness. Jesus was vulnerable at that moment and Satan knew it. Each Satanic gesture was an offer of food, power, and wealth. Jesus, empowered through praying, responded each time with the counsel of scripture (Matthew 4:1–11).

Not only is prayer useful in fighting off demons, but also in sidestepping the dinosaurs that wish to drag us down into irrelevance. Under the guidance of the Holy Spirit, we need inspired and visionary prayers to lead us. Too many of our prayers seem to restrict us to the status quo, missing our need to minister to an increasingly hostile and hurting world, undergoing rapid change. William Easum has emphasized to us that we can't afford to be insensitive to the accelerated pace of change around us; otherwise we are drawn dangerously close to "dancing with dinosaurs."[9] Churches and theological institutions, he suggests, "with a slow pace of change are no longer adequate in a fast-changing world. Structures designed to coordinate ministry are unable to cause innovation. Ministries that worked in the industrial society no longer meet the spiritual needs of people in an informational society. In an age of computers, we cannot express truth in the language of a chariot age. The time has come for new wineskins."[10]

Easum exhorts us to distinguish between essential beliefs that need to be maintained and non-essential practices that we should shed. Prayer can give us perspective; it enables us to face realities that our psyches have not yet accepted. Haven't we already witnessed church buildings turned into furniture stores, restaurants, antique shops, and town houses? Prayer enables us to see these changes and to sound the alarm for renewal. Dinosaurland may already be upon us as we cling to "security," seeking institutional guarantees that can't be made and failing to remember that God's grace is our only guarantee in life. Today, institutional long-range planning teams are confronted with tough choices as schools seek to clarify priorities; the call is out for a new reformation within our communities and faith that is future oriented and realistic. Unless we plan strategically and wisely, we will become a museum of dinosaurs. Canadian writer Douglas Coupland, author of *Generation X*, already anticipates Dinosaurland in his book intentionally entitled *Life after God*.[11]

Finally, the practice of prayer will help us to develop our instinct to find meaning, transcendence, wholeness, and truth.[12] Prayer makes a difference in life by changing our view of the world and our understanding of ourselves. Prayer gives us a cosmic outlook beyond our limited horizons. Through prayer, this instinct for transcendence and wholeness is given an opportunity to express itself; the channels of prayer can lift us to new levels of authenticity and fulfillment beyond our imagination.

Theologian Sallie McFague suggests that all the world is "God's body;" we are all interconnected.[13] Playwright John Guare indicates that there exist only "six degrees of separation" between any two persons on this planet. We are a network of humans who can empower one another by the grace of God through prayer. Spirit-led prayers are essential in quickening the pulse of our theological communities, enabling us to fulfill our mission. Our theological institutions carry the responsibility to support and direct the church's future toward transforming society into the Kingdom of God. Prayer is essential in this transformational process; prayer is indeed at the heart of theological education.

**DISCUSSION STARTER**

Who can be against prayer? Seminary education ought to educate us with wise guidelines on the use and misuse of prayer. Have you ever made a list of the positive and negative uses of prayer? To what extent have we developed a theology of prayer we are willing to share with others within our seminary community? How free are we to discuss prayer on our campuses?

On many campuses there is little evidence that the community is struggling to understand prayer. Perhaps more praying is being practiced than we might think. It's true, seminary communities consist of busy people; time is a premium for us. But is this a valid excuse for neglecting prayer? Are our energies so consumed by other things, no matter how valid, that we have little energy left to express our trust and thanksgiving before God? The more we shift our attention to God, the more liberated we will be in ourselves, enabling us to be more authentic and less guarded in our relationships with one another. When prayer is encouraged without being constricted by conformity, we will energize faculty, students, and staff in our pursuit for theological wisdom and divine direction for our lives. What further steps would enhance our spiritual development and place our intellectual pursuits in perspective? Is there a willingness to relate our faith and our studies regularly through the discipline of prayer?

Chapter 12

# Toward the Ideal Seminary

$C$an you imagine what it would be like to be enrolled or employed at the seminary of your dreams? What is the ideal seminary that will further your journey of faith, enabling you to envision more fully "a new heaven and a new earth?" What is the dream curriculum that will outline adequately the contours of "the new Jerusalem," the Kingdom of God where love, justice, and peace reign? (Revelation 21:1–2).

### A Brief Introduction to "Patch Adams"

The film *Patch Adams,* featuring the actor Robin Williams, has some suggestive lessons for us. In this movie, Patch Adams (Williams) is a second-career medical student seeking to transform the status quo policies at his school. He would like it to become the ideal medical school with a committed faculty who inspire students to become dedicated doctors who will practice medicine with compassion and competency. To that end, he works hard to be the best student he can be (near the top of his class) and at the same time not lose his humanity toward fellow classmates and patients at the hospital. In keeping with the Hippocratic Oath, he strives to do no harm to the patients he encounters, endeavoring at all times to communicate a loving and caring attitude to others, which is what motivated him in the first place to become a physician. But he quickly discovers through the required protocol and policies of the medical school and hospital that his passion for becoming a physician is being squeezed out of him and his fellow classmates.

Physicians, it seems, are sometimes trained to view patients as objects for treatment, not as persons who also have anxieties and fears. He finds the patients often depersonalized by the medical process. By means of humor, he awakens the humanity among patients, hospital staff, and his classmates. His efforts are reprimanded by faculty and administration for violating the rules. Adams, the medical student, was reaching too far "outside the box" for the comfort of the administration at the medical school and hospital. He wanted to reinvent the medical school and hospital as more humane and healthy places—places of *Gesundheit*, meaning, from the German, a healthy, holistic state of mind and spirit, not simply places that discuss and manage the sickly according to a prescribed system.

Adams leads a small cohort of his classmates to establish an alternative model of caring for patients—not an easy task when the allegiance of the establishment is tied to a tenured status quo. There was no effort to encourage innovation or imagination within the medical school community to explore alternative styles of practicing medicine.

## Implications for Theological Education

How does the "Patch Adams" story relate to theological education? If we substitute "seminary" for "medical school" and "church" for "hospital," do we find parallels? Is the theological enterprise too vested in its own status quo processes and academic requirements? What are the correlations between our academic and ecclesiastical processes and the parish expectations for a "qualified pastor"? Do we ever seek conversations with "outsiders" who question our way of doing things? A closed attitude sometimes prevails when attempting to evaluate our educational process for accrediting agencies or when ecclesiastical judicatories request accountability for the actual performance of our graduates in ministry. How often do we view these "outside" interventions as intrusions rather than opportunities for growth and enhancement as a learning organization? To what extent are we willing to risk change when our self-interest and self-image are at stake?

To what degree are campus discussions in our seminaries simply posturing to distance ourselves from persons who desire "a closer walk with God"? Common human needs ought to unite us in our battle against darkness as we grope for direction and authentic spirituality. Today humanity has tasted the emptiness of modernity; many are searching for relief, but aren't finding the necessary nurture and comfort in their churches. They have witnessed for too long now our institutional poverty, lack of passion, hypocrisy, and benign rhetoric for peace and justice while entrapped in the stagnant pools of ecclesiastical and educational conformity.

Have we overlooked the fact that we have entered the ambiguous age of postmodernity, which operates on a digital nervous system constantly surfing cyberspace in search of fulfillment that never seems to last? Wired as we are for new messages, we return to our surfing to discover that the Source of the mystery and meaning of life still evades us. I suspect seminaries are in need of updating our theological maps, to have permission to venture from safe harbors of well-charted theological and biblical interpretations to uncover the broader horizons and galaxies which God beckons us to explore in our journey of faith.

Are we willing to nurture an adventuresome spirit, namely, the will to transcend yesterday's theological boundaries and articulate confessions of faith for a new generation that has little commitment to the past and even less interest in an ecclesiastical culture unwilling to acknowledge youthful aspirations for exploration and recognition? A quote attributed to Albert Einstein claims that, "We cannot solve problems we have created with the same thinking that created them."[1] Isn't such an outlook also a reminder to us in theological education of our own inability to solve problems in our schools using the same approaches and presuppositions that have created them?

A recent book from Bill Gates of Microsoft fame is entitled *Business @ The Speed of Thought*. Gates challenges the business community to update its practices for the Digital Age. Perhaps we in the theological community need a text for ourselves that will challenge us to pursue our primary agenda, *the business of reconciliation @ the speed of divine grace*. Jesus Christ is our Eternal Contemporary, calling us to catch up to him, to experience the liberating power of the gospel that frees us from struggles with yesterday's ecclesiastical vestments. Our task in theological education at the beginning of the twenty-first century is to revive our churches and communities in their journey of faith to the new Jerusalem where justice, kindness and humility exist. (Micah 6:8).

The ideal seminary I envision will model renewal for the churches by constantly reinventing our own delivery of theological education as the Spirit of God leads us through charted and uncharted waters. Seminaries and divinity schools are learning organizations that can't afford to stop experimenting with the learning process, applying what we know and have tested for the benefit of the churches we serve. As an enthused learning community for God, we wish to graduate leaders for our churches who can become change agents who worship God more truly, energized by their theological studies, stimulated by new learning methodologies and innovative service to the community.

Standing at the crossroads between centuries, the mission of theological schools should be focused on reviving our churches; we can no longer take for granted the continuation of denominational churches into the twenty-first century. In some quarters their doom has already been predicated with the rise of megachurches and pentecostalism. It is reported that in 2010, one in every three Christians will be Pentecostal.[2] Let's face it, the health and well-being of traditional seminaries is tied to the health and well-being of traditional churches regardless of any endowments these seminaries might have.

The significance of this linkage should take precedence in determining our priorities and strategic planning for the near future. It should be fundamental to all our educational efforts, as we seek to ignite the embers of our first love for Christ and the church. Theological schools have a leadership role in pointing churches to a new Pentecost. It is the task of the seminary as a graduate school of the church to integrate the dimensions of God's forgiving love and healing so that our churches might be centers of *Gesundheit* before a diseased, violent, and suffering society looking hopelessly for utopias that don't exist.

Imagine with me what an ideal seminary and church might look like that truly welcome rich and poor, the wounded and the ambitious, young and old, single and married, along with the powerful and the weak of whatever race, gender, or ethnic background to our open doors for study, worship, and fellowship. In the ideal seminary as well as the ideal church, we need to practice responsibility for one another's wellness. When the seminary and the church are centers of *Gesundheit*, we will grab the world's attention and respect. No theology, whether it be evangelical, conservative, liberal, or whatever, has credibility with me if it does not practice the love of God in its totality as urged upon us by Jesus the Christ and his example to us.

## Essential Characteristics of an Ideal Seminary

Several essential characteristics of an ideal seminary are necessary to revive and renew our churches. First, the ideal seminary will not waste time discussing the nature of community; instead, its energies will be spent on *being* the community of God, the family of love. Actually, a Christian community of learning calls for more than mutual civility and respect. Differences of opinion and interpretation ought to exist in every learning community, but in the midst of our debates and dialogues let us never lose sight of our common ground in Christ that unites us. In an ideal seminary, diversity of viewpoints is encouraged, not simply diversity of persons. Freedom of expression and inquiry are welcomed. The ideal seminary gives space and permission for asking questions, expressing doubts, sharing crises, testing curiosity, and allowing experiences of forgiveness to take place with one another.

Second, the ideal seminary supports spiritual engagement that is willing to struggle with the holy mysteries of our faith. In an ideal seminary there is no dichotomy between the classroom and the prayer room; in many seminaries, unfortunately, the chapel sees less action than the classroom. For an ideal seminary to become a reality, we need to work on our historic spirituality in order to give balance and perspective to intellectual enquiries.

Third, the ideal seminary would do away with grades and evaluations;

instead we would be so caught up in our desire to please God, that we would expect nothing less from ourselves than our best; this would be our standard. After all, the final evaluation of our lives comes from God, not from one another. When we are truly grateful, what other option is there more fulfilling than offering our finest efforts in gratitude to God who has already accepted us in Christ. In the ideal seminary the atmosphere of thanksgiving prevails, which in turn motivates us to serve God and neighbors with zeal.

Fourth, my ideal seminary would do away with hierarchy in any shape or form. We ought to be united in our common citizenship in Christ, while recognizing at the same time that we are called to different roles and responsibilities within the life of the community. In place of hierarchy, we ought to practice "heterarchy," where everyone feels free to communicate with everyone else.[3] Due largely to our human shortcomings, the seminary and church may not erase hierarchy in your lifetime or mine; nevertheless, heterarchy can be our goal for governance as members of the household of Christ who are baptized into one body—whether Jews or Greeks, employees or volunteers, faculty or administrators, tenured or nontenured, administrative staff or students, we are all heirs to this common citizenship in Christ. When we put competition, fear, and pride behind us, we will become the Body of Christ (1 Corinthians 12:12–31). We must be teachers and students to one another, learning and listening together, building confidence and thereby modeling the seminary's mission to be a true community of God that sends out disciples with a vision for unity within the Body of Christ for the sake of our common mission.

Fifth, the ideal seminary needs to have adequate facilities, be electronically accessible, and have financial support to enable it to minimize scrambling for the scarce resources within the community. In an ideal seminary there would be no need to address constantly the material needs of the seminary community.

Sixth, the ideal seminary will have ingrained in its daily culture the need to share God's love to all, expressed so powerfully in the person of Jesus Christ (John 3:16). The seminary that doesn't exemplify this message in all its dimensions will fail our students and churches in their outreach efforts.

Seventh, the ideal seminary and the ideal church will seriously consider de-emphasizing commencement and confirmation services which often convey that we have "graduated" from further learning. The ideal seminary will have a strong commitment to life-long learning, not only for its clergy but also for its laity. The ideal seminary will provide opportunities for continuing education for *all* of God's people and will provide programs and courses to engage clergy and laity in joint study, worship, and fellowship. In fact, I would like to see a specially designed Master's degree in Christian Leadership to develop lay support. To increase theological education among the laity along with the clergy will contribute immensely to the church's revival and reduce the tendency for clericalism and laicism in the congregation's life.

Eighth, the ideal seminary will, of course, enroll ideal students. This might be more difficult to determine since there is no common consensus between the church and the academy on the profile of an ideal student. For some in the academy, the ideal student is someone who will eventually work on a Ph.D. degree and teach one day in a college or theological school. For the vast majority of us, the ideal student is someone who has intelligence, a creative imagination for ministry, a caring spirit, and leadership qualities that will contribute significantly to the life, nurture, and growth of the congregation, and make a positive impact on the wider community. Most of these traits are God-given gifts that individuals possess and for which the seminary cannot claim credit. We should claim, however, in an ideal seminary, that we send out students with wider horizons than when they entered; we nurture and deepen their love for Christ and the church so that they leave us more excited than ever to energize the church as educated and compassionate leaders who embody and practice the virtues of the Kingdom of God in their communities.

Ninth, the ideal seminary requires an ideal faculty. The profile of an ideal faculty member may have even less consensus among us than the ideal student. Every school will boast of its outstanding faculty. The ideal faculty will point to its list of stimulating teachers, distinguished authors, and extraordinary undertakings. Furthermore, an ideal faculty will communicate and trust one another as it works together to provide an exciting and coherent educational experience that enables students to mature in their faith and enhance the church's witness. The ideal faculty will not limit its influence to their teaching discipline and research agenda, but will also take on wider responsibility for the whole theological enterprise, affirming and empowering not only themselves but every member of the seminary community to do well in our common life together. This is collegiality at its best.

Tenth, the ideal seminary needs an exceptionally dedicated core of administrators and staff to attend to the numerous institutional workings of the seminary community. While it is said that the faculty are the heart of the seminary, it is also true that the administration and staff are the soul of the ideal seminary. Their importance cannot be overstated nor can sufficient gratitude be expressed for the many thankless and hidden tasks they accomplish quietly and efficiently. Theirs too is a calling and concern for the institution and all its members. The ideal seminary is blessed indeed when it has a gifted and committed administration and staff.

Eleventh and last for now, the ideal seminary will also have an ideal Board of Directors backed by a larger number of graduates and friends who believe in the seminary and its mission. Theological education is an extended family affair; the Board of Directors (trustees) of the institution can serve a wise consultative role when they understand the ethos and workings of the school.[4] With their wide range of knowledge and experience, the Board's consultation with the various constituents of the seminary community is beneficial, allowing the Board to develop and interpret policies and strategies wisely that challenge as well as encourage faculty, students, administrators, staff, and donors in fulfilling their responsibilities to advance the seminary's mission.

## Postscript

None of the 243 accredited seminaries and divinity schools within the ATS from my perspective has yet become "the ideal seminary." Having a strong endowment is not sufficient to guarantee an ideal school. All theological institutions with which I am acquainted are actually "works in progress;" I suspect the same can be said of ourselves as individuals. But at least one final factor is necessary to become the ideal seminary: it is our need to energize each other and wish one another well in our respective tasks. Then and only then will the theologies we teach have credibility to revive and renew the church, "making all things new" (Revelation 21:5).

### DISCUSSION STARTER

*H*ow would you characterize the ideal seminary? Are you willing to invest time, effort, and talent to build the ideal theological school in your locale? What impact do you envision cyberspace will have in shaping the ideal seminary? Will in-residence theologizing shift increasingly to the Internet? Or will the ideal seminary of the future be a careful blending of two separate but related delivery systems of theological education?

# Developing a Strategy for Financial Stability

*T*hroughout the pages of this book, I have not discussed seminary finances per se. This was done intentionally. I believe the heart of theological education for each institution rests with the viability of its vision, which seems to get lost in endless discussions over money worries. Each school's self-understanding of its mission is essential if potential supporters are to invest in us. Having clarity about our mission empowers every school to move forward according to its own strategic plan. Developing a strategic, long-range plan is necessary to the educational well-being of our schools. The planning process should allow for constant review and revision.

Having sufficient funds is, of course, an enabling tool to implement strategic plans. Money cannot be ignored, but neither does it rule the day, nor can it capture our imagination and zeal. Money, however, is an important factor in our pursuit for excellence in theological education. We can never take our funding needs for granted; stewardship of these scarce resources calls for accountable reporting to our supporters. If theological schools wish to succeed in their mission, accurate attention to record keeping is required. To assist us in appreciating the importance of having adequate funds, let me share briefly as a case study our seminary's unfolding strategy for financial stability. Doing so should by no means be taken as an endorsement to clone our approach, but rather to recommend that you see it as a means of igniting your imagination to develop a program for financial stability for your institution in keeping with your mission.

## The Situation

In February 1981, when I took up my responsibilities as President and Professor of Theology at Pittsburgh Seminary, the school had in previous years undergone significant downsizing of faculty and administrative staff due to its weakened financial condition. It was actually on a slippery slope dipping into its modest endowment (approximately eleven million) to meet its financial commitments. Coupled with the school's economic instability, there existed also theological confusion over its institutional identity and conflict over styles of leadership within the school. While smoke still lingered in the air from past battles on campus, most of our seminary community was actually worn out and wondering what a theological professor like myself without administrative experience could accomplish in the presidency of the oldest Presbyterian seminary in the Presbyterian Church (U.S.A.).[1] The institution was taking a risk and so was I, motivated as I was by a sense of call and a love for theological education.

Administratively, Pittsburgh Seminary was dysfunctional—the Business Office was in disarray without leadership and an interim Dean was serving who desperately wanted to return to his full-time faculty status; no more than a month into my new responsibilities, the entire boiler system of the seminary collapsed. The trustees on the Finance Committee reluctantly dipped again into the principal of its modest endowment to address the situation, further weakening their financial condition. The Pittsburgh economy at that time was also hurting with unemployment between 15 and 20 percent, due to the enormous reduction of the steel industry that also affected other related business enterprises. One of the knowledgeable business persons on the Finance Committee, a banker, declared in a committee session with his characteristic Presbyterian wisdom, "We will need to prepare ourselves to close Pittsburgh Seminary 'decently and in order.'" Had I come to preside over an institutional funeral?

For the most part, faculty colleagues at the seminary were either unaware of the seriousness of the situation or were hiding behind the illusion that tenure would protect them. It is a rude awakening for faculty to realize that there are limits to the powers of tenure. Even I could see with my naiveté that the outlook was bleak, but theological institutions, like churches, have a tenacity to hold on in spite of numerous shortcomings. Nevertheless, the circumstances at the seminary needed to be addressed quickly, realistically, and strategically in order to provide direction and hope for our future. Frankly, it is difficult to plan for the ideal seminary if your financial need consumes all your energy and time. And that was *the reality* staring me in the face!

## The Strategy

My first step was to stop listening to the "war stories" of the past. The strategy employed could be called "the politics of resurrection." I wanted our seminary to do more than survive; my wish (or vision) was for it to regain a fresh hope and to serve the church as a healthy and viable institution attracting outstanding scholars, students, and support from the grassroots.

Our strategy was twofold in its execution: first, *building the Annual Fund through greater alumni/ae participation in order to increase the number of donor churches and individual giving*, and at the same time engaging the seminary community in physically cleaning up the institution through modest projects; second, *endowment building*.

Operation "clean up" began in the Spring of 1981, shortly after my arrival. I announced to the seminary community that we needed to physically clean our campus as we anticipated our graduation exercises at the end of May. I was also postponing my inauguration until the campus was cleaned up. My faculty colleagues agreed with me to dismiss classes for a designated Spring Cleaning Day. We invited the nearby churches to prepare a picnic supper and join us at the end of that day to celebrate what was accomplished. We painted classrooms, washed walls, and freshened up our campus grounds. It is amazing how much you can accomplish when you have faculty, students, trustees, administrators, and staff all participating—nearly two hundred people working together.

A local newspaper learned of our project and a feature story appeared in the *Pittsburgh Post-Gazette* the following day entitled, "The Seminary Cleans Itself Up." This modest gesture began to open doors for us. It was a good fit with the Presbyterian ethos of Pittsburgh. It signaled to the Pittsburgh community that the Protestant work ethic was alive and well. It also sent a message to our alums that we still cared for the old institution. Today, nearly 50 percent of our alums contribute (more than double from the past) to the Annual Fund; while the total contribution in dollars is not large, coming mainly from pastors of small churches with modest incomes, it sends a signal to church members who tend to follow their example.

Our modest cleanup accomplishments were also looked upon with approval by skeptical and affluent laity who had doubts about the seminary's future and direction. A short time thereafter, a wise businessman challenged us with the first endowment gift of my presidency. *Endowment building was the second important aspect of our twofold strategy.* This businessman's endowment gift of $500,000 was given to enhance our Continuing Education program at the seminary, but he insisted that it had to be matched by an additional $500,000 within a three month period or the gift would be withdrawn. I signed a letter of agreement to his condition as requested, too naïve to entertain the thought that we might not be able to satisfy the challenge. Also, I was very desirous to build the Continuing Education program, which at that time drew approximately three hundred persons to the campus each year. Today our Continuing Education program has well over two thousand clergy and lay persons attending annually some forty-five or more events. We achieved our goal of establishing a $1,000,000 endowment for Continuing Education as the cornerstone of support for our program.

The seminary through Continuing Education presently provides an expanding educational ministry in addition to our regular course work with seminarians. This outreach effort caught the attention of potential donors and also introduced them to our faculty and the needs of our campus. Having a program in place, providing ministry through educational events, led to greater interest in the seminary and financial support. It has been said that "money follows ministry" and I believe it.

With a changing attitude toward the seminary, we began to address the largest area of cost to the seminary budget, namely, the core support of our faculty and academic programs. We thought that the best way to undergird support of our core academic program was to endow faculty chairs that honored both the donor and the faculty incumbent. At the time of my arrival in Pittsburgh, only two named faculty chairs were funded at $350,000 each. *Realistically, there were no fully funded endowed chairs.* The Board of Directors took an assessment of the situation and raised the benchmark from $350,000 to $750,000 and then to $1,000,000 to endow a chair. Currently, our benchmark for an endowed chair is 1.5 million dollars. By the grace of God, we have today twenty fully endowed chairs at Pittsburgh Seminary providing stability to the educational core of our school. This is out of a total of twenty-three faculty, including the President and the Dean.[2]

In addition to faculty chairs, a growing endowment enables us to keep tuition and fees down for our students and to provide them greater financial support during their years at the seminary. As our endowment has increased, we have been able to reduce our percentage of expenditure of endowment earnings from 8.5 percent to approximately 5 percent, more in keeping with the National Association of Colleges and University Business Administrators (NACUBA) guidelines for endowment growth. Ideally, we would like to be at 4.75 percent or less. We have also been able to raise greater grant money for our various outreach programs due in part to our financial stability and commitment to support these programs in the future.

Not to be overlooked beyond endowment monies are the millions of additional dollars that were raised to allow us to remedy many years of neglected maintenance on our buildings and to provide physical renovations to existing facilities to enhance our learning experience and life together as a seminary community. The most recent renovations have been a new dining room and kitchen, a Computer Learning Center, a Physical Fitness Center, expansion of the James L. Kelso Bible Lands Museum, improved acoustics in the chapel, and remodeling of faculty, administration, and staff offices. Our present strategic plans call for additional campus improvements, enhancement of our academic programs, and endowment support for student scholarships.

Financial stability, I believe, also strengthens our academic freedom as an institution. It is often the lack of funds that politicizes us and causes a great deal of anxiety within the educational community. Today, our endowment at Pittsburgh Seminary is approaching one hundred and fifty million dollars. Our budget for 2000–2001 was over 59 percent driven by endowment. Our Annual Fund has also grown from approximately $200,000 to over $740,000 in 2000. We believe the Annual Fund is vitally important to the seminary's long-term stability and flexibility. It also introduces us to a larger mix of donors, some of whom might consider later to contribute to our endowment base as their legacy to the seminary's future educational ministry.

### Are Endowments Healthy for Institutions?

There may be a downside to this success. In the future, the question might well be raised if a large endowment for us or, for that matter, any theological school might cause seminaries to be less accountable and responsive to the needs of the grassroots churches. Endowments can insulate us from the changing needs of the church and perpetuate the status quo concerns of the faculty, administration, and trustees who could be out of touch with grassroots realities. Endowments could cause us to be less flexible, too tied to academic self-interests, vis-à-vis the church's changing needs. A tuition driven institution needs to display a more entrepreneurial spirit (out of necessity) not only to be more responsive to the changing needs of the marketplace but also to generate revenue dollars to run the institution. On the other hand, there is the real possibility that an endowment driven institution could become complacent, less prophetic, and perhaps even less innovative as well. These dangers are real ones, I believe.[3]

Notwithstanding these dangers, a strong endowment can enable us to become responsible players in humanizing a market driven economy. As a significant economic participant, along with our theological analysis of human nature, we can be more realistic and at the same time engaged in relating the gospel to the human situation. We wish to graduate students who understand the gospel within this business-oriented world, who are able to comprehend the limitations of that orientation in their proclamation of the gospel where the disparity and misunderstanding between rich and poor continue to widen.

## Discussion Starter

*L*et me suggest three sets of questions with theological implications for discussion:

First, what are the issues facing your school as you prepare a strategy of financial stability for your institution? Are there issues clearly identified and acknowledged by all parts of the seminary community? The leader's task is to guide the institution in defining *reality* in your situation. Do you have a strategic long-range plan?

Second, to what extent should all funding efforts be viewed as a "calling," acknowledging our daily dependence upon God's grace? In other words, how often is funding approached solely as a development task employing persons, technical methods, and data, while the spirit behind our task is lost? We need to communicate to a seminary community and potential donors that we are *all* engaged in the task of divine development (spiritual formation) that unifies heart, mind, and soul as well as our resources of time, talent, and money into a totality of stewardship before God.

Third, are we educating our seminary communities to the dynamics of a market driven society? Are we teaching ourselves to address those realities with sanctified common sense? An effective prophetic witness requires that we understand the *context* in which we find ourselves. To this end, what reliable data have we gathered and utilized?

# NOTES

### INTRODUCTION: WHY SEMINARY EDUCATION?

1. See Ernest Becker's book, *The Denial of Death* (New York: The Free Press, 1973).
2. Parker J. Palmer, *The Courage to Teach* (San Francisco: Jossey-Bass, 1998), 137.
3. C. S. Calian, *Icon and Pulpit* (Philadelphia: The Westminster Press, 1968), 112–3. See also C. S. Calian, *Theology Without Boundaries: Encounters of Eastern Orthodoxy and Western Tradition* (Louisville: Westminster John Knox Press, 1992).
4. Jackson W. Carroll, Barbara G. Wheeler, Daniel O. Aleshire, and Penny L. Marler, "Harriet Hercon," in *Being There: Culture and Formation in Two Theological Schools* (New York: Oxford University Press, 1997), 125.

### CHAPTER ONE: SEMINARY EDUCATION AND LEADERSHIP

1. See *Bulletin* 43, Part 1, 1998, The Association of Theological Schools in the United States and Canada, Standards of Accreditation under Degree Program Standards, Section A.3.1.3:

> A.3.1.3 *Personal and Spiritual Formation*: The program shall provide opportunities through which the student may grow in personal faith, emotional maturity, moral integrity, and public witness. Ministerial preparation includes concern with the development of capacities—intellectual and affective, individual and corporate, ecclesial and public—that are requisite to a *life of pastoral leadership*. (Italics added.)

> A.3.1.3.1 The program shall provide for spiritual, academic, and vocational counseling and careful reflection on *the role of the minister as leader*, guide, and servant of the faith community. (Italics added.)

> A.3.1.3.2 The program shall provide opportunities to assist students in developing commitment to Christian faith and life (e.g., expressions of justice, *leadership development*, the devotional life, evangelistic witness) in ways consistent with the overall goal and purpose of the school's M.Div. program. (Italics added.)

2. Taken from the prepared remarks of Dr. Aleshire's presentation at ATS 2000 Biennial Meeting in Toronto (June 17–19, 2000) under the theme, "Continuity and Change: The Contexts of Leadership in Theological Schools."
3. Ibid.
4. See Donald E. Miller, *Reinventing American Protestantism: Christianity in the New Millennium* (Berkeley: University of California Press, 1997).

5. From notes taken from Professor Miller's presentation at a retreat in January 2000 in San Diego to Presbyterian seminary presidents and chairs of their Boards of Directors.

6. Aleshire, "Continuity and Change," 14. See also Max DePree, *Leadership Is an Art*, (New York: A Dell Trade Paperback, 1989).

7. Aleshire, "Continuity and Change," 14.

8. See Carroll, et al. *Being There: Culture and Formation in Two Theological Schools* (New York: Oxford University Press, 1997).

9. Daniel Goleman, "Leadership That Gets Results," *Harvard Business Review* (March–April 2000): 78–90. There is a great deal of literature written on leadership. For a review on some of the recent books on leadership, see *In Trust Magazine for Leaders in Theological Education* 2, no. 2 (2000): 28–31. See also John P. Kotter, *On What Leaders Really Do* (Boston: A Harvard Business Review Book, 1999); Edwin H. Friedman, *Reinventing Leadership: Change in an Age of Anxiety* (New York: The Guilford Press, 1996); Michael Maccoby, "Understanding the Difference between Management and Leadership," *The Human Side* (January-February 2000); and Jim Collins, "Level Five Leadership: The Triumph of Humility and Fierce Resolve," *Harvard Business Review* (January 2001): 67–76. For reflections on the leadership role of seminary presidents, see "Leadership: The Study of the Seminary President. Reflections of Seminary Leaders," *Theological Education* 32, suppl. 3 (1996); and Neely D. McCarter, *The President as Educator: A Study of the Seminary Presidency* (Atlanta: Scholars Press, 1996). See also, "The Study of the Seminary Presidency in Catholic Theological Seminaries," *Theological Education* 32, suppl. 1 (1995) and "The Study of the Seminary Presidency in Protestant Seminaries," *Theological Education* 32, suppl. 2 (1995).

10. Goleman, "Leadership That Gets Results," 85.

11. Ibid.

12. Ibid.

13. Ibid., 86.

14. Ibid., 87. See also Robert K. Greenleaf, *The Servant as Leader* (Newtown Centre: Robert K. Greenleaf Center, 1970).

15. If the Association of Theological Schools chooses not to be involved in this way, perhaps the Alban Institute could assume this role. The Alban Institute seeks to connect laity, clergy, and church officials in leadership issues facing churches and communities. Its headquarters are located at 7315 Wisconsin Avenue, Suite 1250 W., Bethesda, MD 20845. E-mail address: InfoCenter@Alban.org.

## CHAPTER TWO: THE SEARCH FOR EXCELLENCE AMONG THEOLOGICAL SCHOOLS

1. *U.S. News and World Report* (April 10, 2000) has an annual list of the best graduate schools in business, law, medicine, engineering, and education for their first professional degree. For theological schools, the first professional degree would be the Master of Divinity degree (M.Div.) for which there is no listing outside of the fact that graduates know that they earned degrees from accredited schools.

2. Based on 1969–70 data, the study entitled *Graduate Education in Religion: A Critical Appraisal* (Missoula: University of Montana Press, 1971), 88–96, cites the top eight schools for doctoral studies in religion. Sponsored by a grant from the American Council of Learned Studies, the project was under the leadership of Dr. Claude Welch.

3. The National Research Council from Washington, D.C. produced a ranking of Ph.D. programs in the United States in 1995. Questions concerning its methodology

raised doubts as to its viability and completeness. A new report is being prepared by the NRC, but it seems they are "unable to make the simple and standard distinctions between ministerial degrees (M.Div., D.Min., etc.) and research degrees (Ph.D.)." Warren G. Frisina, "Qualitative Study Samples Over Doctorates in Theology," *Religious Studies News* 10, no. 4 (November 1995), 29. See also Hugh Davis Graham and Nancy Diamond, "Academic Departments and the Rating Game," *The Chronicle of Higher Education* 45, no. 41 (18 June 1999), 86. The Carnegie Foundation for the Advancement of Teaching has set a new way of restructuring classification of American higher education to broaden "the system's emphasis beyond research funds and discouraging its use as a way to rank colleges." Reported by Julianne Bassinger, "A New Way of Classifying Colleges Elates Some and Perturbs Others," *The Chronicle of Higher Education,* August 2000, A31.

4. See volume edited by Barbara G. Wheeler and Edward Farley, *Shifting Boundaries: Contextual Approaches to the Structure of Theological Education* (Louisville, Ky.: Westminster John Knox Press, 1991).

5. See "The Good Theological School," discussed in *Theological Education* 30, no. 2 (Spring 1994). We should reflect on what Daniel O. Aleshire, currently the Executive Director of the Association of Theological Schools, says about accreditation and standards: "Accreditation should assure the public that certain things are true about an accredited institution, but beyond this, accreditation should help a school to envision an upward trajectory, an institutional goal, an institutional capacity to improve. If redeveloped ATS standards only broaden the floor, or redefine minimally acceptable levels of operation, they contribute little to quality in theological education, and, ultimately, little to the good of the religious communities served by theological schools." See also *Characteristics of Excellence: Standards for Accreditation (Draft for Discussion)*, Middle States Commission on Higher Education (February 14, 2001).

6. See Gilbert Bilezikian, *Community 101* (Grand Rapids: Zondervan Publishing House, 1997).

7. See Elizabeth A. Dreyer, "Excellence in the Professions: What Theological Schools Can Learn from Law, Business, and Medical Schools," *Theological Education* 33, no. 1 (Autumn 1996), 1–21. Note also the supporting comment on relationships from Rebecca S. Chopp: "But if knowing God is as much a matter of right relationships as it is a mastery of correct ideas, then the present crisis of theological education cannot be fixed merely by reordering the curriculum. New relationships of imagination, of justice, of dialogue must be found in the midst of a pluralistic world and new forms of relating, teaching, and community building will have to be developed. The *how* of learning is directly related, in this notion of theological education as a process, to the *what* of learning. Indeed, the task for the subjects of theological education may be as much the doing of new forms of relationships to God, self, others, traditions, and society as it is the articulation of right ideas." Rebecca S. Chopp, *Saving Work: Feminist Practices of Theological Education* (Louisville, Ky.: Westminster John Knox Press, 1995), 3.

## CHAPTER THREE: ACADEMIC FREEDOM AND SEMINARY EDUCATION

1. For text, see G. L. Joughin, ed., *Academic Freedom and Tenure: A Handbook of the American Association of University Professors* (Madison: University of Wisconsin, 1969), 33–39. According to an *In Trust* survey (Autumn 1998), 11, approximately two-thirds of the membership of the Association of Theological Schools offer tenure; the

remaining one-third offer contracts. This particular issue of *In Trust* is devoted to a discussion of academic tenure.

2. Actually, it sometimes comes as a shock to faculty members when their school is in such serious financial trouble that tenure proves to be no real protection at all. Establishing endowed faculty chairs, not tenure, may be a more substantial way of providing both financial security and status to a faculty member.

3. "Academic Tenure Policy at Pittsburgh Theological Seminary," adopted by the Board of Directors (November 11, 1981).

4. *Academe* (January–February 1998), 61. See also in the same issue of *Academe*, Martin E. Marty's keen observations on the topic of the AAUP conference under the heading, "In the Crossfire between Academic and Religious Freedom," pp. 63–67. Another thoughtful essay is by Robert N. Bellah entitled, "Freedom, Coercion, and Authority," *Academe* (January–February 1999), 17–21. See also Nicholas Walterstorff's article, "Ivory Tower or Holy Mountain? Faith and Academic Freedom," *Academe* (January–February 2001), 17–22. There are also other related articles in this issue of *Academe* under the general theme, "Religion and the Academy."

5. See Patricia A. Hollander's article, "Evaluating Tenured Professors," *Chronicle of Higher Education,* 17 June 1992, 44. See also the related article by Cary Nelson entitled, "The Real Problem with Tenure Is Incompetent Faculty Hiring," *Chronicle of Higher Education,* 14 November 1997, 84–85. Further articles on tenure and academic excellence that are helpful include: Linda Carroll, "Tenure and Academic Excellence," *Academe* (May–June 2000); and in the same issue, Matthew W. Finkin's "The Campaign Against Tenure," 20–21.

6. For a fuller discussion, see Richard P. Chait's "The Future of Academic Tenure," *Priorities,* no. 3 (Spring 1995).

7. "Procedures, Standards, and Criteria for Membership," ATS *Bulletin* 4, part 3.

## CHAPTER FOUR: WHO OWNS THE SEMINARY?

1. According to the research of Elizabeth Lynn and Barbara G. Wheeler, the public considers theological schools to be "invisible institutions that produce leaders who offer little civic or public leadership." "Missing Connections," *Auburn Studies,* no. 6 (September 1999), 1.

2. David H. Kelsey, *To Understand God Truly: What's Theological About A Theological School* (Louisville: Westminster John Knox Press, 1995).

3. See the discussion in *Auburn Studies* already cited and note also the contributions by Harold Dean Trulear, "Prophecy and Presence," 24–28; Richard J. Mouw, "What Is Our Business?" 17–19; and Jeremiah McCarthy, "A Distinctive Voice," 29–31.

4. See Robert D. Putnam, *Bowling Alone: The Collapse and Revival of American Community* (New York: Simon & Schuster, 2000). Also see the review by Mark Chaves, "Are We 'Bowling Alone' and Does It Matter?" *The Christian Century,* 19–26 July 2000, 754–756. See also Jürgen Moltmann, *Theology of Hope* (London: SCM Press, 1965); and C. S. Calian, *Berdyaev's Philosophy of Hope* (Minneapolis: Augsburg Publishing House, 1968).

## CHAPTER FIVE: TOMORROW'S SEMINARY CURRICULUM

1. Edward Farley, *Theologia: The Fragmentation and Unity of Theological Education* (Philadelphia: Fortress Press, 1994).

2. "Toward Theological Understanding: An Interview with Edward Farley," *The Christian Century,* 4–11 February 1998, 113.

3. Ibid.

4. C. S. Calian, *Where's the Passion for Excellence in the Church?: Shaping Discipline Through Ministry and Theological Education* (Wilton, Conn.: Morehouse Publishing, 1989), 60.

5. Peter Hodgson, *God's Wisdom: Toward a Theology of Education* (Louisville, Ky.: Westminster John Knox Press, 1999); as well as Professor Farley's works already cited.

6. "Toward Theological Understanding," 115.

7. For a recent and much broader discussion of this concern, see Dorothy Bass, ed., *Practicing Our Faith: A Way of Life for a Searching People* (San Francisco: Jossey-Bass, 1997). See also Craig Dykstra, *Growing in the Faith: Education and Christian Practice* (Louisville, Ky.: Geneva Press, 1999).

8. See Roy Floyd, "An Interfaith Dialogue on Forgiveness: Introduction," *The World of Forgiveness* (Periodical of the International Forgiveness Institute, September/October, 1998). The Institute's address is: P.O. Box 6153, Madison, WI, 53716-0153.

9. Desmond Tutu, "A Chance to Begin Again," *Spirituality and Health* (Winter 1999), 29. See also Michael Battle, *The Wisdom of Desmond Tutu* (Louisville, Ky.: Westminster John Knox Press, 1998), A18-A20.

10. Tutu, "A Chance to Begin Again," 29.

11. Donald W. Shriver, *An Ethic for Enemies: Forgiveness in Politics* (New York: Oxford University Press, 1995). See also David Van Biema, "Should All Be Forgiven?" *Time Magazine,* 5 April 1999, 55–58; and Scott Heller, "Emerging Field of Forgiveness Studies Explores How We Let Go of Grudges," *The Chronicle of Higher Education,* 17 July 1998.

## CHAPTER SIX: MAKING THE WORLD YOUR CLASSROOM

1. Robert Banks, *Reenvisioning Theological Education: Exploring a Missional Alternative to Current Models* (Grand Rapids: Wm. B. Eerdmans Publishing Co., 1999), 268. See also works by Darrell L. Guder, *Be My Witnesses: The Church's Mission, Message, and Messengers* (Grand Rapids: Wm. B. Eerdmans Publishing Co., 1985); *The Continuing Compassion of the Church* (Grand Rapids: Wm. B. Eerdmans Publishing Co., 2000); and edited by Guder, *Missional Church: A Vision for the Sending of the Church in North America* (Grand Rapids: Wm. B. Eerdmans Publishing Co., 1998); and George Hunsberger and Craig Van Gelder, *The Church Between Gospel and Culture* (Grand Rapids: Wm. B. Eerdmans Publishing Co., 1996).

2. Banks, *Reenvisioning Theological Education,* 142, 144.

3. Ibid., 144.

4. We have sought to do this through three outreach activities: our Metro-Urban Institute, the Center for Business, Religion, and Public Life, and the World Mission Initiative. In addition, we offer a more general list of continuing education events for clergy and laity. More information on all of these programs is available. Our Web site is: www.pts.edu.

5. Ibid., 143. Banks summarizes these models of theological education. See also Peter S. Hodgson, *God's Wisdom: Toward a Theology of Education* (Louisville, Ky.: Westminster John Knox Press, 1999).

CHAPTER SEVEN: THE GLOBALIZATION AND
MULTICULTURALIZATION OF THEOLOGICAL EDUCATION

1. See ATS *Bulletin* 43, Part 1 (1998) on globalization:

3.2.4.1 Theological teaching, learning, and research require patterns of institutional and educational practice that contribute to an awareness and appreciation of global interconnectedness and interdependence, particularly as they relate to the mission of the church. These patterns are intended to enhance the ways institutions participate in the ecumenical, dialogical, evangelistic, and justice efforts of the church. The term *globalization* has been used to identify these patterns and practices collectively.

3.2.4.2 Globalization is cultivated by curricular attention to cross-cultural issues, as well as the study of other major religions; by opportunities for cross-cultural experience; by the composition of the faculty, governing board, and student body; by professional development of faculty members; and by the design of community activities and worship.

3.2.4.3 Schools shall develop practices of teaching, learning, and research (comprehensively understood as theological scholarship) that encourage global awareness and responsiveness.

See additionally, *Handbook of Accreditation*, Section 7, "Guidelines for Evaluating Globalization in ATS Schools." For more information, contact ATS at 10 Summit Park Drive, Pittsburgh, PA, 15275-1103 or call (412) 788-6505.

2. This reality of interconnectedness is particularly seen when theological schools include programs on urban ministry that involve the entire learning community. Urban ministry "presents some of the most complex and challenging opportunities for seminarians, pastors, and congregations. This means that for urban theological education to be authentic in its engagement and reflection it must be theoretical, global, missional, spiritual, polycultural, prophetic, collaborative, empowering, and transforming. Any one or combination of these can become a paradigmatic lens for examining a particular urban phenomenon." Warren Denis, Katie Day, and Ron Peters, "Urban Theological Education: A Conversation About Curriculum," *Theological Education* 34, no. 1 (Autumn 1997), 49.

3. See the informative article by Dale T. Irvin of the New York Theological Seminary entitled, "Open-Ended Pedagogy in a Multicultural Classroom: The Case for Theological Education," supplement to *Religious Studies News* 2.1 (February 1996), under the "Spotlight on Teaching" section. See also the survey conducted among ATS schools in 1998 by Judith A. Berlong, "Our Words Are Beginning to Make It So: ATS Schools on Cross-Cultural Relationships and Globalization," *Theological Education* 36, no. 2 (Spring 2000), 63–80.

4. Ivrin, "Open-Ended Pedagogy in a Multicultural Classroom."

CHAPTER EIGHT: EXPANDING
THE HORIZONS OF SEMINARY EDUCATION

1. Loren Mead, "Power and Ownership in the Church: Clericalism, Institutional Authority, Lay Participation," *In Trust* 10, no. 9 (Spring 1999), 21.

2. Ibid., 22. See "True and False: The First in a Series of Reports from a Study of Theological School Faculty," *Auburn Studies,* no. 4 (January 1996), 4.

3. We are in the process of witnessing this shift at Pittsburgh Seminary where our continuing education programs for clergy and laity have gone from 300 persons two decades ago to over 2000 now attending events annually. Equally exciting is our "After 4 Program" that invites laity to take seminary classes with seminarians after work, joining the seminary's growing evening degree programs. Unfortunately, these lay persons are part-time students and to date, not eligible for the same benefits that full-time seminarians receive. Hopefully, we will establish a scholarship program for laity and educate ourselves and donors to the shift from a primary "clerical paradigm" of seminary education to a "people of God paradigm" that would be a representation of the whole church.

4. See "True and False," 4.

5. See the persuasive argument on behalf of computer technology set forth in Nicholas Negroponte's book, *Being Digital* (New York: Random House Vintage Books, 1995). Professor Negroponte is on the faculty of Massachusetts Institute of Technology (MIT) and is founding director of the Media Lab. See also Quentin J. Schultze, "Going Digital," *The Christian Century,* 31 January 2001, 16–21; and Lorne L. Dawson, "Doing Religion in Cyberspace: The Promise and the Perils," *Bulletin* (February 2001), 3–9. The *Bulletin* is published by the Council of Societies for the Study of Religion.

6. Negroponte, *Being Digital,* 229.

7. Reported by Jeffrey R. Young, "David Noble's Battle to Defend the 'Sacred Space' of the Classroom," *The Chronicle of Higher Education,* 31 March 2000, A47.

8. Ibid.

9. Ibid., A48.

10. See Section F, Distance Education under Procedure V, "Procedures for Approval of Programs Involving Multiple Location (Exterior Sites) and Distance Education," *ATS Bulletin* 44, Part 1 (2000), 31–32.

11. Jeffery R. Young, "Moving the Seminar Table to the Computer Screen," *The Chronicle of Higher Education,* 7 July 2000, A34.

12. Sarah Carr, "Princeton, Stanford, and Yale Plan Alliance to Offer Online Courses to Alumni," *The Chronicle of Higher Education,* 17 March 2000, A47. See also Raymond B. Williams, "Getting Technical," *The Christian Century* 7–14 February 2001, 14–18.

13. See *Theological Education* 36, no. 1 (Autumn 1999), devoted to "Educational Technology and Distance Education: Issues and Implications for Theological Education." In this issue, it is reported by Katherine Amos of the ATS staff that of the 201 schools that responded to an ATS Distance Education Survey, sixty-two schools reported that they were involved in some form of distance education, while one hundred thirty-four reported that they were not involved in distance education (p. 127). For a fuller discussion, see her "Report of the Survey of ATS Schools on Educational Technology and Distance Education," pp. 125 140. According to Harvard University Professor Chris Dede, no one will be discussing the pros and cons of distance education in ten years. It will be commonplace in the educational process, just one more method to enhance teaching and learning, bringing the whole world closer to the student. Eleanor Chute, "Virtual Schools Open Doors," *Pittsburgh Post-Gazette,* 29 August 2000, A1 and A10.

14. C. S. Calian, *Survival or Revival: Ten Keys to Church Vitality* (Louisville, Ky.: Westminster John Knox Press, 1998), 1. See also the following thoughtful articles: Quentin J. Schultze, "Lost in the Digital Cosmos," *The Christian Century,* 16 February 2000, 178–183; and John R. Thropp, "Can There Be a Virtual Church?" *The Clergy Journal* 26, no. 5 (March 2000), 4–7.

## CHAPTER NINE: WHO IS QUALIFIED TO MINISTER?

1. Nanette Sexton Ross, *Horizons: The Newsletter of the Fund for Theological Education* 3, no. 2 (Spring 2000), 1. For an earlier study on student profiles, see Ellis L. Larson, "A Profile of Contemporary Seminarians Revisited," *Theological Education* 31, suppl. (1995). See also Barbara Wheeler, "Is There a Problem? Results from a Survey of Seminary Students," *The Presbyterian Outlook,* 18 September 2000, 10–13.

2. For more information on the efforts of the Fund for Theological Education (FTE), contact their office at: 825 Houston Mill Road, Suite 250, Atlanta, GA 30329-4211, or email at: fte@thefund.org.

3. Wheeler, "Is There a Problem?" 1–3. See also Robert Banks, *Reenvisioning Theological Education,* especially his chapter, "Reconfiguring the Student Profile," 189–198. See also Calian, "Characteristics of Excellence in Clergy Leadership," Chapter 6 in *The Passion for Excellence in the Church,* 41-44.

4. Steve Levin, "Seminaries See a Graying of the Pulpit," *Pittsburgh Post-Gazette,* 28 May 2000, A1 and A19. See also Valerie Marchant, "Why Not Teach Next?," *Time,* 29 May 2000, G1–G3.

5. A copy of the survey may be requested from the Fund for Theological Education Web site at: www.thefund.org. See also Barbara G. Wheeler's article, "Fit for Ministry?," *The Christian Century,* 11 April 2001, 16–23.

6. Daniel Goleman, *Emotional Intelligence* (New York: Bantam, 1995).

7. Ibid. Professor Goleman offers a fuller explanation of emotional intelligence in his book.

8. See Sarah E. Hinlicky's article, "Seminary Society," *First Things* (August/September 2000): 14–16, on her reflections after entering seminary.

## CHAPTER TEN: GOING THROUGH SEMINARY WITHOUT LOSING YOUR FAITH

1. H. Richard Niebuhr, *The Meaning of Revelation* (New York: Macmillan Co., 1941), 47.

2. Schubert Ogden, "What Is Theology?," *The Journal of Religion* 32, no. 1, (January 1972), 28.

3. "Report of Task Force on Spiritual Development," *Theological Education* 3, no. 3 (Spring 1972), 159–197. Written over three decades ago, it fits today's contemporary scene as well.

4. Nicolas Berdyaev, *Truth and Revelation* (New York: Harper & Brothers, 1955), 58. See also C. S. Calian, *The Significance of Eschatology in the Thoughts of Nicolas Berdyaev* (Leiden: E. J. Brill, 1963).

5. Niebuhr, *The Meaning of Revelation,* 77.

6. John Calvin, *Institutes of the Christian Religion,* Library of Christian Classics, 20, ed. John T. McNeill (Philadelphia: The Westminster Press, 1960), Book III, ch. 2, 551.

## CHAPTER ELEVEN: THE PLACE OF PRAYER IN SEMINARY EDUCATION

1. Eugene Peterson, *The Message* (Colorado Springs: Nav Press, 1995), 646–48.
2. Ibid.

3. See Vladimir Lossky, *The Mystical Theology of the Eastern Church* (London: James Clarke & Co., 1957) and C. S. Calian, *Theology Without Boundaries.*

4. Abraham Heschel, *God in Search of Man* (New York: Farrar, Straus & Cudahy, 1955), 28.

5. Ibid., 375.

6. William James, *The Varieties of Religious Experience* (New York: Macmillan Publishing Co., 1902), 464.

7. See Augustine, *Confessions* (London: Penguin Books, 1961), 21. Augustine's complete statement reads as follows: "The thought of you stirs him so deeply that he cannot be content unless he praises you, because you made us for yourself and our hearts find no peace until they rest in you."

8. Karl Barth, *Prayer: According to the Catechism of the Reformation* (Philadelphia: Westminster Press, 1952) 9–10.

9. William Easum, *Dancing with Dinosaurs* (Nashville: Abingdon Press, 1993).

10. Ibid., 13

11. Douglas Coupland, *Life after God* (New York: Simon & Schuster, 1995).

12. Arianna Huffington, *The Fourth Instinct: The Call of the Soul* (New York: Simon & Schuster, 1995), 14.

13. Sallie McFague, *The Body of God* (Minneapolis: Fortress Press, 1993), 210–11.

### CHAPTER TWELVE: TOWARD THE IDEAL SEMINARY

1. See C. S. Calian, *Survival or Revival: Ten Keys to Church Vitality* (Louisville, Ky.: Westminster John Knox Press, 1998), 132.

2. See Harvey Cox, *Fire from Heaven: The Rise of Pentecostal Spirituality and the Reshaping of Religion in the Twenty First Century* (Reading, Mass.: Addison-Wesley Publishing Co., 1995).

3. Michael Maccoby, "Creating Network Competence," *The Human Side* (May–June 2000), 59. Dr. Maccoby is a specialist on the behavior of profit and non-profit organizations. "In this age of learning," for Maccoby, "heterarchical competence is essential for success" (60). Before a learning organization can gain this competence, "it must learn the principle of effective dialogue" (Ibid.). Two books to get us started are Daniel Yankelovich, *The Magic of Dialogue* (New York: Simon & Schuster, 1999) and Peter Senge, *The Fifth Discipline* (New York: Doubleday, 1998). Maccoby's newsletter, *The Human Side*, may be obtained from the Maccoby Group, PC, 1 Farragut Square South, Suite 704, Washington, D.C. 20006-4003. Their home page is: www.maccoby.com. See also the focused dialogue on the future of theological education in the new millennium as seen from the perspective of former ATS presidents in *Theological Education* 36, no. 2 (Spring 2000).

4. See *The Good Steward: A Guide to Theological School Trusteeship* (Washington, D.C.: Association of Governing Boards [AGB], 1983).

### AFTERWORD

1. If interested, see James Arthur Walther, ed., *Ever a Frontier: The Bicentennial History of The Pittsburgh Theological Seminary* (Grand Rapids: Wm. B. Eerdmans Publishing Co., 1994). Pittsburgh Seminary was founded in 1794.

2. See also Bob Bettson's article, "Rehabilitation, Renewal, and Resources," *In Trust*, 11, no. 4 (Summer 2000). Bettson discusses views of Pittsburgh Seminary's strategy for economic stability.

3. The following are some salient features on endowments in higher education from the American Council on Education in a booklet entitled, *Understanding College and University Endowments* (Washington, D.C.: ACE, 2000):

Most public colleges and universities have no endowments or only nominal amounts.

Two-thirds of private institutions have endowments of less than $5 million.

The median endowment at private colleges and universities is roughly $10 million, which at a typical spending rate would support an annual expenditure of only about $500,000.

Of the nation's 3,706 colleges and universities, only 368—about 10 percent—have endowments over $50 million.

Of the thirty-four institutions with endowments exceeding $1 billion, twenty-six are private and eight are public. Of the one hundred largest endowments, roughly one-third are at public universities.

In addition to colleges and universities, other institutions with endowments include churches, hospitals, museums, private secondary schools, and performing arts groups.

# BIBLIOGRAPHY

Allen, Diogenes. *Spiritual Theology: The Theology of Yesterday for Spiritual Help Today*. Boston: Cowley Publications, 1997.

Banks, Robert. *Reenvisioning Theological Education: Exploring a Missional Alternative to Current Models*. Grand Rapids: Wm. B. Eerdmans Publishing Co., 1999.

Bass, Dorothy C., ed. *Practicing Our Faith: A Way of Life for a Searching People*. San Francisco: Jossey-Bass, 1997.

Browning, Don, David Polk, and Ian Evison, eds. *The Education of the Practical Theologian: Responses to Joseph Hough and John Cobb's Christian Identity and Theological Education*. Atlanta: Scholars Press, 1989.

Calian, Carnegie Samuel. *Today's Pastor in Tomorrow's World*. Philadelphia: The Westminster Press, 1982.

_____. *Where's the Passion for Excellence in the Church?* Wilton, Conn.: Morehouse Publishing Co., 1989.

_____. *Theology Without Boundaries: Encounters of Eastern Orthodoxy and Western Tradition*. Louisville, Ky.: Westminster John Knox Press, 1992.

_____. *Survival or Revival: Ten Keys to Church Vitality*. Louisville, Ky.: Westminster John Knox Press, 1998.

Carroll, Jackson W., Barbara Wheeler, Daniel Aleshire, and Penny Long Masler. *Being There: Culture and Formation in Two Theological Schools*. New York: Oxford University Press, 1997.

Carter, Stephen L. *The Culture of Disbelief: How American Law and Politics Trivialize Religious Devotion*. New York: Basic Books, 1993.

_____. *Integrity*. New York: Basic Books, 1996.

Chopp, Rebecca S. *Saving Work: Feminist Practices of Theological Education*. Louisville, Ky.: Westminster John Knox Press, 1995.

Cladis, George. *Leading the Team-Based Church: How Pastors and Church Staffs Can Grow Together into a Powerful Fellowship of Leaders*. San Francisco: Jossey-Bass, 1999.

Dykstra, Craig. *Growing in the Life of Faith: Education and Christian Practicing*. Louisville, Ky.: Geneva Press, 1999.

Farley, Edward. *Theologia: The Fragmentation and Unity of Theological Education*. Philadelphia: Fortress Press, 1994.

Farley, Edward and Barbara G. Wheeler, eds. *Shifting Boundaries: Contextual Approaches to the Structures of Theological Education*. Louisville, Ky.: Westminster John Knox Press, 1991.

Fisher, James L. *Power of the Presidency.* New York: Macmillan Publishing Co., 1984.

Gardner, John W. *Self-Renewal: The Individual and the Innovative Society,* rev. ed. New York: W. W. Norton & Co., 1981.

Hamel, Gary and C. K. Prahalad. *Competing for the Future.* Boston: Harvard Business School Press, 1994.

Hodgson, Peter C. A. *God's Wisdom: Toward a Theology of Education.* Louisville, Ky.: Westminster John Knox Press, 1999.

Hough , Joseph and John Cobb. *Christian Identity and Theological Education.* Chico, Calif.: Scholars Press, 1985.

Jinkins, Michael and Deborah Bradshaw Jinkins. *The Character of Leadership: Political Realism and Public Virtue in Nonprofit Organizations.* San Francisco: Jossey-Bass, 1998.

_____. *The Good Steward: A Guide to Theological School Trusteeship.* Washington, D.C.: Association of Governing Boards (AGB), 1983.

Kelsey, David. *To Understand God Truly: What's Theological about a Theological School.* Louisville, Ky.: Westminster John Knox Press, 1992.

Kerr, Clark, ed. *Presidents Make a Difference: Strengthening Leadership in Colleges and Universities.* Washington, D.C.: Association of Governing Boards, 1984.

Kitagawa, Joseph M., ed. *Religious Studies, Theological Studies and the University Divinity School.* Atlanta: Scholars Press, 1992.

Leith, John. *Crisis in the Church: The Plight of Theological Education.* Louisville, Ky.: Westminster John Knox Press, 1997.

McLean, Jeanne P. *Leading from the Center: The Emerging Role of the Chief Academic Officer in Theological Schools.* Atlanta: Scholars Press, 1999.

Miller, Glenn T. *Piety and Intellect: The Aims and Purposes of Ante-Bellum Theological Education.* Atlanta: Scholars Press, 1985.

Muller, Richard A. *The Study of Theology: From Biblical Interpretation to Contemporary Formulation.* Grand Rapids: Zondervan Publishing House, 1991.

Oswald, Roy. *Finding Leaders for Tomorrow's Churches: The Growing Crisis in Clergy Recruitment.* Washington, D.C.: Alban Institute, 1993.

Pacala, Leon. *The Role of ATS in Theological Education 1980-1990.* Atlanta: Scholars Press, 1998.

Sanneh, Lamin. *Translating the Message: The Missionary Impact on Culture.* New York: Orbis Books, 1996.

Schuller, David S. *Ministry in America.* New York: Harper & Row, 1980.

Senge, Peter. *The Fifth Discipline: The Art and Practice of the Learning Organization.* New York: Doubleday, 1990.

Smith, Page. *Killing the Spirit: Higher Education in America.* New York: Penguin Books, 1989.

Stackhouse, Max. *Apologia: Contextualization, Globalization, and Mission in Theological Education.* Grand Rapids: Wm. B. Eerdmans Publishing Co., 1994.

Thistlewaite, Susan B. and George F. Cairns, eds., *Beyond Theological Tourism: Mentoring as a Grassroots Approach to Theological Education.* Maryknoll, N.Y.: Orbis Books, 1994.

Thistlewaite, Susan B. and Mary Potter Engel. *Lift Every Voice: Constructing Christian Theologies from the Underside,* rev. ed. Maryknoll, N.Y.: Orbis Books, 1998.

Wood, Charles M. *Vision and Discernment: An Orientation in Theological Study.*
    Atlanta: Scholars Press, 1987.
Yates, Wilson. *The Arts in Theological Education: New Possibilities for Integration.*
    Atlanta: Scholars Press, 1990.

# ACKNOWLEDGMENTS

*I* have been blessed with a wonderful "editorial team" of supporters consisting of my wife, Doris, who for the past forty years has assisted me faithfully through the important editing process before publication; my secretary Linda Smith gives conscientious support in so many ways; Elizabeth Miles prepared and typed the manuscript when Linda broke her wrist; my brother-in-law Charles DeMirjian provided his creative input and critical questioning; Executive Editor Stephanie Egnotovich added wisdom, encouragement, and constructive suggestions, and President and Publisher Davis Perkins of Westminster John Knox Press affirmed my intentions throughout this project. My thanks to the staff of the Barbour Library at Pittsburgh Theological Seminary for their resourcefulness and to Ellen Little and Anita Johnson for their added assistance.

I would be remiss if I did not express my appreciation to the loving members of my family, especially to grandchildren Rachel, Paula, Luke, Caleb, and Sam for their patience with Grandpa who was not always as available as he should have been during the writing of this book. The needed renewal of theological education is for the sake of these grandchildren and generations to come.

# INDEX

135